RESURRECTION LIFE NOW!

How to Rise Above It All
and Live Life to the Fullest

Anne Gimenez

Harrison House Publishers

Tulsa, Oklahoma

16 15 14 13 12   10 9 8 7 6 5 4 3 2 1

Resurrection Life Now!
How to Rise Above It All and Live Life to the Fullest
ISBN: 1-978-160683-665-1
Copyright © 2012 by Gimenez Evangelistic Association
P.O. Box 61777
Virginia Beach, VA 23466

Published by Harrison House
P.O. Box 35035
Tulsa, OK 74153
www.harrisonhouse.com

Table of Contents

Foreword:

Mothers teach their daughters many things. My mother, like so many, worked all my life to teach me the essence of being a Godly and honorable woman. How to pray, read my Bible, tell the truth, have integrity and most importantly, be true to who God called me to be.
Cooking and cleaning didn't seem to be the focus of my training. As I traveled with my parents, I saw the true meaning of living what you preach. My parents were true examples to me that preaching the word was not only a calling, but it was our way of life.

My mom use to tell me, "Robin, if anything ever happens to me (referring to her health), don't let me go to the hospital with all my jewelry on. We may never get it back. Do you understand?" Now this, to a young kid, seemed crazy. "Why are youtelling me this?" I wanted to say. "Nothing is gonna happen to you!" Looking back, as a young person, when you know that your parents are living for God, doing everything they know He is calling them to do, they are invincible super heroes in your eyes.

So when I found myself standing over my mother at 5:30 a.m. on January 23, 2010, in Palm Beach, Florida, It felt like a dream. "This isn't suppose to be happening! Not to my mother! She's invincible!" All these things raced through my mind as I began taking off her jewelry. "What are you doing?", she asked. "This is where we take your jewelry off, mom." She looked at me with hollow and trusting eyes and said "ok". I heard the paramedics coming down the hall as I raced to get her rings and necklaces off, but couldn't get her earrings off in time. I felt like I had failed in my first task, but I was determined not to fail at the next.

I followed the ambulance to the hospital and as soon as I got there, I was taken in to fill out all the paperwork. Once finished, I raced through the double doors into the emergency room. A small woman in a lab coat asked, "Are you Anne Gimenez's family?" "Yes, I'm her daughter", I replied. "She's been sent to the heart lab. I'm afraid she's had a heart attack and it doesn't look like she's going to make it." Suddenly I couldn't breathe. I struggled to keep the room from spinning as I processed what she said. Then, as if realizing that I had been trained for this moment, I looked into the doctors eyes and said, "She has not had a heart attack, and she is NOT dying!" And so the journey with my mother and the battle for her healing began.

I went into ICU and found my mom's room. They had put her in an induced coma, and had her hooked up to a respirator and several IV machines. The nurse told me that they were starting her on a heart attack protocol. "What do you mean a heart attack protocol?" I asked. "She hasn't had a heart attack!" The nurse began to tell me that she understood that it was hard to accept reality, but I needed to get a grip on this because I needed to make some decisions and sign some papers. "I'm not signing anything until you change that protocol!" I demanded. "Your mother has had a heart attack!" the nurse insisted. "No she hasn't! Get the doctor back in here!" I shouted. "If you want the doctor, you can call him yourself." the nurse replied walking away. I went to the nurses station and asked for my mother's cardiologist. As I dialed the phone, I asked the Lord, "Are you here? Do you see us? My mother has lived her life according to your word. She's done everything you have ever asked her to do without question.
Please fight for her! Help me fight for her! We need your help right now!" I talked to the doctor and there was no heart attack; the nurses were mistaken and they entered my mom's room and began changing things quickly. The "heart attack protocol" could have killed her! As they hung the new bags of medications and checked the monitors, I sat there thinking, this can't be happening. I had just lost my father 2 years earlier and I couldn't even begin to think about losing my mother too.

By that night, her kidneys had failed. She was showing signs of infection and they couldn't figure out where. "Her heart can't take this." the on-call doctor said. "She can't survive the night." By that time, my husband, John, had arrived with some of the elders from our church. My mom's assistant and another of our assistant pastors had also arrived. We had all gone into pray for mom and anoint her with oil. I was doing everything I had been taught and trained to do. But I was scared. I was making life and death decisions, and I knew it. They had started her on 24 hour dialysis and several antibiotics. A nurse was assigned to sit with her around the clock adjusting IV's and monitoring the respirator. By the next morning, her liver had failed. They still couldn't figure out what was causing the infection and her heart was losing more and more function. But she had lived through the first night!

One morning after several days, I was having my morning talk with the Lord telling Him all the things that the doctors were saying. "Her heart is functioning at only 10%, her liver and kidneys have failed, her blood pressure is too low." I immediately heard the Lord say to me in a strong voice, "Don't believe anything you see, and don't believe anything you hear. You are only to believe in what I say!" I was stunned! I looked in the mirror and determined that morning, that I was no longer going to listen to their reports. I would only lean on what God said over my mother's life.

After meeting with her cardiologist, pulmonary specialist, oncologist, hematologist, internist, gastroenterologist, urologist and infectious disease specialist, one thing was clear, they had no clue what was happening to my mother. Her body was shutting down and they didn't know why. The more they tested, the more they were confused. But she was still alive, and we were still fighting. After she came out of the coma, we had her moved to a bigger hospital with better treatment where she was diagnosed with viral myocarditis which is an often fatal condition in which a virus attacks your heart. There, she began the long road to recovery that included a lot of therapy.

One day the therapist asked me, "what appliances does your mother usually use?" I was confused. I asked "what do you mean?" "Does she normally use a walker or a cane?" "My mom?" I laughed. "My mom stomps around in three inch heals everyday and preaches at least twice a week at church!" I chimed. "Her high heels are the only appliances she uses!"

A few days later I transferred her to a live-in rehab center. She started progressing quickly through her rehab. One day I got a phone call. "Mrs. Blanchard?" "yes", I replied. "You need to come pick your mother up." "What do you mean I need to pick her up?", I said. "She's too independent to remain in the rehab center. If she's gonna dress herself, shower herself, wheel herself around and walk in and out of the bathroom by herself, she may as well be with you. Come pick her up." When I got there, mom was already packing her stuff. "I'm ready to go!" she said. So we gathered up the rest of her things and headed back to the apartment.

After three and a half months of being gone, I was ready to go home! On the way to the airport, my mom turned to me and said, "I'm not taking the wheelchair with me. I won't need it." We arrived home April 23rd and on July 4th, Independence Day, she preached her first message back at the church. I'll never forget that message. She entitled it "Unfulfilled Promises"

A year later, mom went to see the cardiologist that saved her life in Dallas. He did a complete check up on her and was astounded by her progress. "You have a resurrected heart!" he proclaimed. "No limitations. You can do anything you want to. Your heart can take it!"

When mom emerged out of this trial, she did so with a new zeal for life and for preaching the word. Many have said to me, "Your mom looks incredible!" I always smile and say, "She is incredible!" When people see her, they cannot believe what she has been through. Just a few years ago, they told me she'd need a liver, kidney and heart transplant. "You don't come back from this type of illness!", the doctors said over and over. BUT GOD!

I received a NOW word like Abraham. In Gen. 22:12 The angel of the Lord said to Abraham, "Lay not thine hand upon the lad..." Abraham didn't hold on to the old word but received a NOW word that caused him to obey God's purpose.

There are many times in our lives that we face an impossible situation, like Abraham did. Like my mother and I did. But like Abraham, God was faithful to give me a NOW word. "Don't believe anything you see and don't believe anything you hear". That was my NOW word. 1 Corinthians 2:9 says "... Eye hath not seen, nor ear heard, neither have entered into the heart of man, the things which God hath prepared for them that love him." I now realize that the doctors and nurses could not comprehend the things that God had prepared for my mother. But I could. I knew He had unfinished plans for her.

As a little girl, I remember my mother getting on the floor behind the dining room table to pray. Listening to her for hours as she bombarded the throne room of God. The times she would tell me what God was speaking to her and I'd ask her how she knew God said that. She would teach me about trying the spirit and listening for that still small voice. She taught me how to seek God, listen for his leading. Not to hesitate when he spoke and walk in faith, believing He would do what he said.

I know that God raised my mother up from her deathbed to bring this message of Resurrection Life NOW to the body of Christ. She has lived it! This is not just a revelation from the word, this message is a revelation from her life. The message in this book is real and it is true. Resurrection life can be yours NOW....Today! And although circumstances and reports may lead you to believe that things can't turn around. Hold on to your NOW word and believe that the Resurrection Life God has promised is yours NOW!

-Robin Gimenez Blanchard

"But if the Spirit of him that raised up Jesus from the dead dwell in you, he that raised up Christ from the dead shall also quicken your mortal bodies by his Spirit that dwelleth in you." Romans 8:11

Preface

You may have noticed that this old world is rocking and reeling like a drunken sailor. The news is filled with turmoil and violence in every area of society, and now even the United States seems to be in tremendous upheaval. From foreign affairs to our economy, from Wall Street to Main Street, our lives are being hit with all kinds of trials and trouble.

A lot of people don't know what to do or which way to turn. Maybe that's you. Or maybe you know pretty much what God has called you to do, but you are having a terrible time trying to do it. You take a leap of faith, and instead of landing on your feet, you find yourself bottoms up! You press forward two steps and get pushed back three steps.

You know what I'm going to say: Jesus is still the answer. And that's true! However, in this book we are going to explore the reality of what that means to you right now, living on planet Earth, facing the world in which you live. After all, if Jesus doesn't make a difference, then we all might just as well sit down and quit. If this Christian life doesn't work, there are things we'd rather be doing than praying prayers that are never answered and preaching a Gospel that makes no difference in our lives or the lives of people around us.

I believe the problem is that we don't know *how* Jesus is the answer. We say it like mindless parrots—"Jesus is the answer! Jesus is the answer!"—but we either have forgotten or have never comprehended that in Christ Jesus we have a life of power. And it's not just any kind of power. This is power beyond fossil fuel, electrical, or nuclear power. This is power that raises dead things to life! Resurrection power for a resurrection life.

Resurrection life is how Jesus is the answer.

We must understand and walk in this truth, or should we just sleep through the rest of our lives, getting whatever pleasure we can find and hoping we don't have too many bumps in the road? Beloved, I know that is not what you want for your life! Nor do you want that for your family, friends, co-workers, and neighbors. If you did, you wouldn't be reading this book.

You are reading this book because God wants you to know and I'm here to tell you that you can have an extraordinary life in Christ Jesus. You can overcome the world and fulfill your divine destiny. You can crucify your carnal desires and live only according to God's desires for your life. You can plow new ground and do amazing exploits. But in order to do all these things, you must grab hold of His Resurrection Life Now!

Chapter 1

Resurrection Life Before You

"For I know the plans I have for you," says the Lord. "They are plans for good and not for disaster, to give you a future and a hope."

Jeremiah 29:11 NLT

I realized something interesting one day while I was studying the Word. This revelation has had a profound effect on everything I believe about God's plan for my life. Suddenly, I was swept away by the understanding that God "had my back" way before I was even a thought in my parents' minds. His resurrection life was released into my life long before I was born, and His resurrection life is set before me in my future. I just have to apprehend that ancient and absolute truth and walk in it today. And because God is no respecter of persons, He has resurrection life built into the plan for your life too.

You Are No Accident!

What I realized that day was that the word "before" has two meanings. It can indicate something that happened in the past or something that is ahead of us. We could say, "That happened before we were born," or we could say, "A great adventure lies before us." When something from God was before, it means you must reach back to comprehend it, study it, and take hold of it. When something from God is before you, you must reach forward to obtain it. And in this case, the resurrection life He has for you was ordained before and is set before you at the same time.

The apostle Paul says in Philippians 3:13, "Brethren, I do not count myself to have apprehended." He is saying that he is reaching for something that is before him, or in front of him, and he has not grasped it yet. He goes on to say, "But one thing I do." What is the one thing he does to apprehend the plan of God for his life? "Forgetting those things which are behind…." In this context, Paul is telling us to forget our sins, our failures, and the wrong thinking that will keep us from taking hold of what God has for us in our present and our future.

Remember Lot's wife? The Lord told Lot and his family not to look back at Sodom when they fled for their lives, but Lot's wife looked back and instantly turned into a pillar of salt (Genesis 19:26). She just had to take one last, lingering look at a place that epitomized sin, lawlessness, and complete rebellion against God. This tells us two things: You had better reverence and obey God (especially when you're running for your life), and you won't fulfill His plan for your life if you love the sins of your past more than Him.

You cannot go forward with God in this hour and continually look back. You can't go over the past or pray about the past and change it. That's a prayer God cannot answer. The past won't change! What's done is done, and it can't be undone. If you have terrible things in your past, if you have done things you actually enjoyed for awhile and still feel tempted by them (like Lot's wife), God will give you the grace to overcome those things as you reach for the things He has before you! Forget what's behind you. Let it go!

Resurrection Life Before You

Then Paul says, "… and reaching forward to those things which are ahead…." We are to reach forth, to stretch out and extend ourselves as much as we possibly can. In verse 14 he says, "I press." I love this, because when I looked it up in the Greek, "press" means "to run swiftly in order to catch a person or thing."[1] In other words, you see what's before you and make a run for it.

"I press toward the goal." The King James Version says, "I press toward the mark." What's the mark? What's our goal? It's to become a mature believer in the body of Christ, living in resurrection life now. That's what we press into. We're making a run for Jesus! Whenever anyone looks at us and examines our lives, we want to be "marked" by the character and works of the Lord Jesus Christ. That is our goal.

Paul ends this verse with, "…for the prize of the upward call of God in Christ Jesus." Are you called? We talk about that a lot, but to be called means to be invited[2]; our calling is a high calling because God is calling us upward. The place He has called us to inhabit is a higher place. And what is the prize? Resurrection life! You and I have been invited to live in a higher dimension—spiritually, mentally, emotionally, and physically—and it's called resurrection life.

When you were born from above by the Spirit of God, you became a true Jew (Romans 2:29), a child of God through the blood of Jesus the Messiah. You are no longer a "mere human being" like everybody else on this Earth. You are a new creature in Christ Jesus (2 Corinthians 5:17). I like to say God has transformed you from a barnyard chicken to an eagle saint! Being born again by the Spirit of God, now you live and exist and move and have your being in another dimension, a dimension of God's character and power. You're in Christ and have His resurrection life in you. Hallelujah!

Resurrection Life Now!

When the apostle Paul spoke of not looking back, He was referring specifically to the past sins and failures that we can't do anything about. I think you realize there is nothing you can do to change the past. No prayer will do that. However, there is also something fantastic in your past that will never change.

We speak the wisdom of God.

1 Corinthians 2:7

The wisdom of God is the plan of God. Do you know, God's not walking around in Heaven, scratching His head, and saying, "What am I going to do with you? Shall I send you to the beach, or do I need to put you in the library?" No, He's had your life all mapped out for a long, long time. He didn't just make up a plan for you when your mama got pregnant with you. It didn't just come to His mind when you were born. His plan is an eternal plan.

"What are you saying, Pastor Anne?"

I'm saying that what God said to Jeremiah, He is saying to you right now:

"Before I formed you in the womb I knew you; Before you were born I sanctified you; I ordained you a prophet to the nations."

Jeremiah 1:5

You may not be called to be a prophet, but the rest of the verse is for you! As Jeremiah grew up and became a prophet to the nations, most likely his friends and relatives said, "Oh, Jeremiah, before you is a great ministry." Now remember that "before you" can be that which happened in the past or that which will happen in the future. It can be behind us or ahead of us. So Jeremiah would tell them the word of the Lord. He would say, "You don't understand. I was a prophet before. I was a prophet before I was ever born. Before I was even conceived in my mother's womb, God knew me. He knew the person I would be and everything I would do." God knew you before in the same way He knew Jeremiah.

Now let's read the rest of 1 Corinthians 2:7:

But we speak the wisdom of God in a mystery, the hidden wisdom which God ordained before the ages for our glory.

The hidden wisdom of God was His plan for you, which He made before the ages. Before time was created, in eternity past, God ordered your steps. Before time ever began, He had a plan for you that would be inspired and empowered by His resurrection life. Your life today was ordered and established before the ages.

You are not an accident in the mind and heart of God!

Nothing Can Stop God's Plan for You—Except You

Then God said, "Let Us make man in Our image, according to Our likeness; let them have dominion over the fish of the sea, over the birds of the air, and over the cattle, over all the earth and over every creeping thing that creeps on the earth."

Genesis 1:26

At this point in Genesis, time had started, but God didn't just come up with the idea of making man in His image. First Corinthians 2:7 says He already knew what He was going to do before time began. I will tell you from the Word of God and from my experience: Nothing is going to stop the plan of God in your life except you. You can choose to serve yourself and the devil instead of God. You can choose to worship another fallen human being or your profession or a hobby. You can choose not to receive Jesus as your Lord and Savior. But if you choose to be saved and serve God all your life, there is no way God's amazing plan for your life can be stopped!

Resurrection Life Now!

So let's just picture God, sitting there before He created time, planning the ages to come and all the lives of the people who would love Him and serve Him with their whole hearts. God said, "Let Us make man in Our image." Did you notice that He refers to Himself in the plural? Was God talking to Himself? Was He crazy? No! This reveals the Father, the Son, and the Holy Spirit were all a part of the master plan.

Of course, we know "man" refers to mankind. Initially, that was Adam and Eve. God had a plan for each one of us before time ever began. He had a blueprint. This tells me there is one thing in the past that I can reach for, that I can extend myself to obtain: The plan for my life that God ordained before He ever made the Earth I stand upon. While I am reaching for the things that are before me, I am also reaching for the things that were before me. I'm reaching for that eternal plan and divine destiny that is mine in Christ Jesus. I'm reaching for who I am becoming and what I am doing—all that God ordained from before time.

I didn't decide I was going to be the pastor of Rock Church. The truth is, I never even got to decide I was going to be a woman preacher. God decided I would preach and I would pastor. If it had been up to me, I probably wouldn't have chosen that calling. Let me tell you, back when He called me, there were almost no women preachers and pastors. It was hard! I used to say, "God calls mostly men, but He calls a few women just to show you He can do it if He wants to."

When I began preaching and then when I became a pastor, I had to reach back into eternity past and grab hold of what God had ordained for me. I had to know in my spirit that, without a doubt, this was what I was created to do. With that ancient truth abiding deep in my heart, with what had gone before me, I could embrace what was before me in my future—the good, the bad, and the glorious!

Resurrection Life Before You

If you read the Bible, there are some pretty powerful women preachers and pastors in both the Old Testament and the New Testament. And the New Testament really seals the deal by stating that in Christ Jesus there's neither male nor female (Galatians 3:28). So I preach and I pastor because I know it is scriptural. I can confidently reach back to apprehend and comprehend the things God ordained for me from before the foundation of the world; and at the same time, I am fully secure in reaching forward to obtain the things He has before me.

And we know that all things work together for good to those who love God, to those who are the called according to His purpose.

Romans 8:28

Do you love God? Are you called (invited) by Him to join Him in His purpose, His plan for you and all His children, His plan for the earth? Let the redeemed of the Lord say so! Choose to live for Him. Choose to follow Jesus, who is the author and finisher of your faith (Hebrews 12:2). I won't tell you it's easy, but I will tell you without a doubt that you will never regret it. Why? Because when you choose to follow Jesus, He will infuse you with resurrection life.

The Alpha and Omega

He chose us in Him before the foundation of the world.

Ephesians 1:3

Do you know that everything in your life begins and ends with Jesus? He chose you before the foundation of the world, and now you follow Him in everything He has set before you. Long before time began, He called out your name and beckoned you to come to Him, to be God's child and participate in His kingdom. When He walked on earth He told you a great deal about His kingdom and the part you would play.

Resurrection Life Now!

"Therefore every scribe instructed concerning the kingdom of heaven is like a householder who brings out of his treasure things new and old."

Matthew 13:52

The kingdom of Heaven is God's spiritual realm, and as His children we have been given rule and dominion in that spiritual realm. We are "householders." We actually live in the kingdom of God. This means we have a treasure, or we might call it God's treasury, which has old and new things for our use. We can dip into this treasury and pull out whatever we need—including the ancient truths from eternity past that give us a road map to the new things in our future. I like how the New Living Translation translates Matthew 13:52:

"Every teacher of religious law who becomes a disciple in the Kingdom of Heaven is like a homeowner who brings from his storeroom new gems of truth as well as old."

Sometimes I preach a truth I haven't heard from anyone else or read in a book. But as I am teaching God's Word, the Holy Spirit will tell me something or show me something, and I share it. One of those truths is the theme of this book. I realized that God's resurrection life was granted to me before the foundation of the world; at the same time, His resurrection life is before me, waiting for me to tap into it. His resurrection life is the prize by which I attain to the character and high calling of God my Father. And I have all this because of Jesus.

Right now I'm reaching for the ancient things as well as the neverheard-of things. I want to know God's purpose and plan. I want to know every intimate detail of the covenant that was made between the Father and the Son before the earth and the galaxies were ever formed, the covenant I was born into by His Spirit and am walking in today. Before time began they agreed that the Son would come to this earth and be the sacrifice for the sins of all people.

Resurrection Life Before You

All who dwell on the earth will worship him, ... the Lamb slain from the foundation of the world.

Revelation 13:8

In the mind and plan of God, Jesus was offered up on the cross long before He entered Mary's womb. God never went to Plan B when Adam fell. He knew Adam was going to sin against Him and die spiritually. He knew mankind would be lost in their trespasses and sins forever unless His Son became human and paid the debt for sin. That was Plan A, decided from before the foundation of the world, and He never left Plan A. And so the Lamb was slain before the foundation of the world. Before.

God kept this plan a mystery until Jesus was resurrected. Then the cat was out of the bag! The Bible says there was a good reason for this:

But we speak the wisdom of God in a mystery, the hidden wisdom which God ordained before the ages for our glory, which none of the rulers of this age knew; for had they known, they would not have crucified the Lord of glory.

1 Corinthians 2:7-8

If the devil had known what would happen because of Jesus being crucified, he never would have crucified Him. He would have given Him mouth-to-mouth resuscitation and commanded Him not to die! But God kept the truth hidden from the devil, although Jesus did hint at it a few times. This just shows you how dense Satan really is.

But Jesus answered them, saying, "The hour has come that the Son of Man should be glorified. Most assuredly, I say to you, unless a grain of wheat falls into the ground and dies, it remains alone; but if it dies, it produces much grain.

John 12:23-24

Resurrection Life Now!

If Satan had put two and two together, he would have figured out that Jesus would multiply Himself by dying. Then His body of saints would give Him more glory than ever. Truly, if the devil had gotten this, he would have pleaded, "Please don't die!" But he never figured it out.

We saints, on the other hand, have the ability of God in us to understand what was and what is before us:

> But as it is written: "Eye has not seen, nor ear heard, Nor have entered into the heart of man the things which God has prepared for those who love Him." But God has revealed them to us through His Spirit. For the Spirit searches all things, yes, the deep things of God.
>
> 1 Corinthians 2:9-10

We have the Spirit of God in us, and He enables us to understand the mysteries of God. He is the resurrection life in us that is revealing what was before us and what is before us. We may be surprised when He tells us what was and is before us! But we won't be surprised when it happens, because we have the resurrection life of the Spirit, who has revealed it to us.

> And now, O Father, glorify Me together with Yourself, with the glory which I had with You before the world was.
>
> John 17:5

Before the world was, Jesus was slain. He wasn't created when He was born of Mary. Before time began, He was the Son of the Living God and lived in Heaven with the Father. He was at the meeting when the covenant was decided. He knew what was before Him: the Cross and the resurrection. He didn't become a human being just to experience human life. He emptied Himself of everything that He was and took a robe of clay in order to die on the cross, pay the debt for our sins, and make a way for us to get back into the family of God.

Jesus did it all for you and me. He wanted us that badly!

Paul exhorts us:

Therefore do not be ashamed of the testimony of our Lord, nor of me His prisoner, but share with me in the sufferings for the gospel according to the power of God, who has saved us and called us with a holy calling, not according to our works, but according to His own purpose and grace which was given to us in Christ Jesus before time began.

2 Timothy 1:8-9

Before time began! Everything that is before you in Christ Jesus was before you in Christ Jesus. The Father, the Son, and the Holy Spirit knew your name, what you would look like, and how you would see the world. God knew your family line, everything you would inherit from them, and all your experiences with them. He knew all the sins and failures and mistakes you would make. And what did He do? The Father made a covenant in His Son's blood for you so that you could have the resurrection life of His Spirit.

... in hope of eternal life which God, who cannot lie, promised before time began.

Titus 1:2

Before time began. The Son came to this earth, and when He was twelve years old, Jesus said, "I must be about my Father's business" (Luke 2:49). He had a job to do. He showed us the heart of the Father by healing the sick, raising the dead, providing food and clothing for the poor, and calming the wind and the waves. He walked on water and cast out demons. He revealed the mind of God by preaching and teaching. But none of these things were the main event.

"Now My soul is troubled, and what shall I say? 'Father, save Me from this hour'? But for this purpose I came to this hour. Father, glorify Your name."

John 12:27-28

His purpose was to die on that cross of Calvary so that you and I could be forgiven of our sin, become God's children, and live in His presence forever. In Adam we lost the way, but then Jesus Christ came saying, "I am the way. I'm the way back to God."

"For truly against Your holy Servant Jesus, whom You anointed, both Herod and Pontius Pilate, with the Gentiles and the people of Israel, were gathered together to do whatever Your hand and Your purpose determined before to be done."

Acts 4:27-28

The Father, the Son, and the Holy Spirit "determined before" what was going to happen to the Son after He became Jesus of Nazareth, and Jesus knew it.

He indeed was foreordained before the foundation of the world, but was manifest in these last times for you.

1 Peter 1:20

What does foreordained mean? It was decided before it actually happened. It was predetermined. Another biblical word for this is predestined. For many years Christians didn't want you to talk or preach about being predestined, and yet it's all through the Bible. The Word says Jesus was predestined, and you and I were too. Although we aren't perfect and the devil will do everything he can to stop us, we can fulfill the call of God on our lives. Why do I think that? Because Jesus was foreordained and so are we!

The Bible says Jesus endured the cross for "the joy that was set before Him" (Hebrews 12:2), and His joy was you and me! He went through the rejection, the beatings, the whipping, and the excruciatingly painful death of crucifixion because He knew what was foreordained. Not only would He be resurrected, but He was going to bring you and me right along with Him. The cross was the legal means to our resurrection life!

Your Resurrection Life

I've heard people say, "I just hate God."

I just can't help myself, and I have to answer them, "Are you insane? Honey, He's the one who's keeping you alive! And if you will give your life to Him, you will find out how He planned a great life for you way before time began." The honest truth is this: The only reason people hate God is because they know He's out there, they know He's calling them, and they don't want to serve Him. They want to serve themselves. They want Him to do what they want Him to do instead of trusting Him with their lives. They blame Him for every bad thing that happens to them and pat themselves on the back when good things happen. Truthfully, they are living in darkness and death. They are missing the amazing resurrection life He wants to give them.

I love God for many reasons. One of them is that I know I'm here by divine purpose. I do what I do in the kingdom because that's what the Father, the Son, and the Holy Spirit planned for me from before the foundation of the world. When I was a little girl and someone would tell me hello, I would say, "I'm called to preach."

"How do you know you're called to preach?"

"I just know it."

"How long have you known it?"

"All my life."

I had never seen a woman preacher. Never heard of one. I just knew down inside, where we know the ancient truths that have been foreordained in the Lord Jesus Christ and are now set before us to walk in.

You have a purpose too. You may not know it yet. You may not understand it yet. Or maybe you know it and you are fighting it and running from it. Maybe you are wrestling with fulfilling it. I'm talking about what God planned for you from before the foundation of the earth and what He has set before you—they are the same!

For we are his workmanship, created in Christ Jesus unto good works, which God hath before ordained that we should walk in them.

Ephesians 2:10 KJV

I was riding on a train when I was single many years ago. My mother and I had been visiting a potential "suitor" in California. As we travelled east, across Arizona and New Mexico toward our home in Texas, I gazed out the window and thought, *I wonder what God has for my future.* Just then, I heard Ephesians 2:9 in my spirit, "Eye has not seen. Ear has not heard. Neither has it entered into the heart the things that God has prepared for those that love Him." And then I heard, "And this is not what I have prepared for you." I knew I was not going to move to California. That was not what He had prepared for me from before the foundation of the world, so it was not set before me.

Sometimes we are disappointed when God turns us a different direction than where we want to go. That's because we just haven't caught on yet to the greater picture He has for us. He sees the end from the beginning. He knew us before time began, and He knows the absolute best purpose and plan for our lives in our time. He can see our resurrection life before—past, present, and future.

Don't ever be fooled into thinking the will of God will always be something you're going to love or that it will be easy! Proverbs 3:6 says to acknowledge God in all our ways, then He will direct us. That's easy to do when I'm going where I want to go and doing what I want to do, but when I'm in situations I don't like, sometimes I have to acknowledge the Lord through clenched teeth! I've said, "Evidently, this is Your will for me, because if I could change it, I would. But I know You have put me here, and I'm acknowledging You. I'm also going to give thanks to You for it, because that's what the Bible tells me to do." (See 1 Thessalonians 5:18.)

It takes all my courage and strength to do this, but when I do, I feel everything inside me change. The circumstances are still the same, but I am different. Now I know what makes that difference: His resurrection life! It has been patiently waiting through eons of time, after being released from before the foundation of the world, waiting for me to come on the scene, receive Jesus as my Savior, and move forward in faith and power.

When you live from what God ordained before and trust Him as you set about doing all He's set before you to do, the fullness of His character and power will fill you to overflowing. You actually walk in His resurrection life—and that makes you a miracle-working miracle!

Resurrection Life Now!

Chapter 2

Resurrection Life Saves You

I once read a story about a man and his wife who traveled the world seeking knowledge and truth. They got an audience with the Dalai Lama, and they found themselves enveloped in a hum. They realized that all around them Buddhist monks were praying, so they asked the Dalai Lama what was going on inside these men when they prayed. His answer was that their prayer was effective if they felt right when they prayed.

People ask me, "Can people who aren't Christians pray and experience God? Isn't it really God who answers them, even if they aren't praying to Him in Jesus' name? I mean, if something supernatural happens to them, and if they feel spiritually lifted up when they pray, aren't they tapping into what we Christians are experiencing spiritually?"

Not according to the Bible. Romans 8:9 says, "Now if anyone does not have the Spirit of Christ, he is not His." If those Buddhist monks, for example, were feeling anything spiritual, they were feeling another spirit, because they had never given their lives to the Lord Jesus Christ. I will go one step further and say that if anyone does not have the Spirit of Christ living inside them, they are not spiritually alive; they are spiritually dead.

Resurrection Life Now!

The difference between those monks and a true believer in the Lord Jesus Christ is the monks' hum is dead while a believer's prayer is alive with resurrection power, a power that brings dead things to life! When the monks pray, they pray to a dead god with no power; the believer in the Lord Jesus Christ prays to a God who is alive and omnipotent, all-powerful. In fact, He died and was resurrected three days later, and now He lives forever in Heaven interceding for them.

Our God is alive!

What Are You Supposed to Believe?

We call ourselves believers, but what are we supposed to believe? That Jesus died for us on the cross? That we are forgiven and going to Heaven? That the entire Bible is the Word of God? I was amazed to discover that it is a lot simpler than I thought.

Now after the Sabbath, as the first day of the week began to dawn, Mary Magdalene and the other Mary came to see the tomb. And behold, there was a great earthquake; for an angel of the Lord descended from heaven, and came and rolled back the stone from the door, and sat on it. His countenance was like lightning, and his clothing as white as snow. And the guards shook for fear of him, and became like dead men.

But the angel answered and said to the women, "Do not be afraid, for I know that you seek Jesus who was crucified. He is not here; for He is risen, as He said. Come, see the place where the Lord lay. And go quickly and tell His disciples that He is risen from the dead, and indeed He is going before you into Galilee; there you will see Him. Behold, I have told you."

So they went out quickly from the tomb with fear and great joy, and ran to bring His disciples word.

And as they went to tell His disciples, behold, Jesus met them, saying, "Rejoice!" So they came and held Him by the feet and worshiped Him. Then Jesus said to them, "Do not be afraid. Go and tell My brethren to go to Galilee, and there they will see Me."

Matthew 28:1-10

Jesus of Nazareth did just what He said He was going to do: He died for our sins on the cross and then was raised from the dead three days later to give us resurrection life. He is the Messiah, the anointed Savior and resurrected Lord of all those who will receive Him. In fact, the Bible tells us that the resurrection was the proof that Jesus of Nazareth was the Son of God, the sinless Holy One, and therefore qualified to die on the cross for the sin of mankind.

... His Son Jesus Christ our Lord, who was born of the seed of David according to the flesh, and declared to be the Son of God with power according to the Spirit of holiness, by the resurrection from the dead.

Romans 1:3-4

The women came early to His tomb and saw that the massive stone had been moved from the doorway and that Jesus' body was gone. Then the angel told them (my paraphrase), "He's not here. He has risen and is alive! So go tell the disciples that they will see Him in Galilee."

The women believed. What did they believe? What made them believers? They believed Jesus had risen from the dead, that He was alive forevermore. The other disciples, on the other hand, were not so quick to believe. Here is how the Gospels report it:

Then the eleven disciples went away into Galilee, to the mountain which Jesus had appointed for them. When they saw Him, they worshiped Him; but some doubted.

Matthew 28:16

Now when He rose early on the first day of the week, He appeared first to Mary Magdalene, out of whom He had cast seven demons. She went and told those who had been with Him, as they mourned and wept. And when they heard that He was alive and had been seen by her, they did not believe.

After that, He appeared in another form to two of them as they walked and went into the country. And they went and told it to the rest, but they did not believe them either.

Later He appeared to the eleven as they sat at the table; and He rebuked their unbelief and hardness of heart, because they did not believe those who had seen Him after He had risen.

Mark 16:9-14

It was Mary Magdalene, Joanna, Mary the mother of James, and the other women with them, who told these things to the apostles. And their words seemed to them like idle tales, and they did not believe them. But Peter arose and ran to the tomb; and stooping down, he saw the linen cloths lying by themselves; and he departed, marveling to himself at what had happened.

Luke 24:10-12

The Gospel of John records the famous account of "Doubting Thomas":

Now Thomas, called the Twin, one of the twelve, was not with them when Jesus came. The other disciples therefore said to him,

"We have seen the Lord."

So he said to them, "Unless I see in His hands the print of the nails, and put my finger into the print of the nails, and put my hand into His side, I will not believe."

And after eight days His disciples were again inside, and Thomas with them. Jesus came, the doors being shut, and stood in the midst, and said, "Peace to you!" Then He said to Thomas, "Reach your finger here, and look at My hands; and reach your hand here, and put it into My side. Do not be unbelieving, but believing."

And Thomas answered and said to Him, "My Lord and my God!"

Jesus said to him, "Thomas, because you have seen Me, you have believed. Blessed are those who have not seen and yet have believed."

John 20:24-29

These last words of Jesus to Thomas are exactly what we are to believe: Jesus of Nazareth was resurrected from the dead three days after He was crucified. And when we believe this, like Thomas we cry out, "My Lord and my God!" We are believers!

If you read through each gospel account of what happened after the women found the empty tomb, you will see that Jesus had to appear to His own disciples, the ones He had walked with for three years, several times before they really believed He was their risen Lord. But He said to Thomas that those of us who would never actually see Him in His resurrected body and yet still believe—simply by the Word of God and the conviction of the Holy Spirit—would be blessed. I don't know many people who have seen Jesus in the flesh today, so that makes most believers today blessed of the Lord, including you and me!

Resurrection Life Now!

I will tell you something else that makes me shake with gratitude every time I think about it: If Jesus isn't alive, you and I don't have any hope for this life or the next. If He only died on the cross for us, shedding His blood for our forgiveness, but He didn't rise again, we would be forgiven sinners, but we would not be righteous. We wouldn't have eternal life or resurrection life. I'm so glad He is alive!

All spiritual and physical blessings pivot on the belief that Jesus was resurrected. If you don't believe He's alive and well and on the throne, exercising all authority and power as the King of kings and Lord of lords, you're just believing in a religion. I think that's why so many people don't have as much fun as the believers I know do. They just have a religion called Christianity; they don't have a living, breathing, walking, talking Savior who is their partner in life, who supernaturally strengthens them and gives them wisdom and guidance, who is their resurrection life! That's why believers are blessed. Jesus is alive to them and He's alive in them!

What do believers believe? Jesus is alive!

The Cross Was Not a Disaster

For if when we were enemies we were reconciled to God through the death of His Son....

Romans 5:10

The death of God's Son wasn't something that never should have happened. People with no clue to the truth would blame the disciples. "They should have taken better care of Him. He needed better security. They should have figured out what Judas was up to and found a way to avoid Jesus being arrested in the first place. After all, the Jewish leaders had been after Him for a long time."

Resurrection Life Saves You

That wasn't the case at all. Jesus said,

"I lay down My life that I may take it again. No one takes it from Me, but I lay it down of Myself. I have power to lay it down, and I have power to take it again."

John 10:17-18

The Son of God came into this world to give His life and shed His sinless blood so that sinners might be forgiven and born again. We use the terms "saved" and "reconciled to God." He saved us from eternal damnation and brought us back into the presence and family of the Father. If you don't know how all this came about, let me tell you the greatest story ever told.

God created Adam and Eve in His image, which means they were created to live forever in health and prosperity in every area of their lives. God created human beings for life, not death! But their quality of life was dependent upon intimate, daily fellowship with the Godhead: Father, Son, and Holy Spirit, who are the source of all life.

God never created human beings to be sick and die or to be dead to Him spiritually. We are His beloved children. He wants to know us and to be close to us, and He created us to want to know Him and to be close to Him. That's the only way we will be completely happy and at peace inside.

However, God always gives human beings the choice to live for Him or for themselves, so He put the Tree of the Knowledge of Good and Evil in the Garden of Eden and told Adam and Eve not to eat the fruit of it. You know what happened. They ate the forbidden fruit and fell from glory into sin. Spiritually, they were separated from God and His eternal life, and eventually they died physically as well.

Resurrection Life Now!

God held Adam responsible because Adam was the head of the human family. He was created first. Through him, all his descendants were separated from the life of God, and that included you and me. Our sins condemned us to eternal death and damnation. However, we saw in the last chapter that God already had a plan to help us get back to Him and to be made righteous! Hallelujah! He had a blueprint already laid out to free us from eternal death and bring us back into eternal life, and that blueprint was the Cross and the resurrection of His Son.

> *Therefore, as through one man's offense [Adam's] judgment came to all men, resulting in condemnation, even so through one Man's [Jesus'] righteous act the free gift came to all men, resulting in justification of life. For as by one man's [Adam's] disobedience many were made sinners, so also by one Man's [Jesus'] obedience many will be made righteous.*
>
> *Romans 5:18-19 [inserts mine]*

Through Adam, sin and death reigned over mankind until the Son of God became a human being, Jesus of Nazareth. Jesus died on the cross for Adam's original sin and the sins of every person who ever lived or would live. How do we know this is what Jesus accomplished? What is our proof? We know our sins were paid for and we now can have peace with God through His shed blood because Jesus was raised from the dead (Romans 1:3-4).

Legally, God could never have raised Jesus up if He had ever sinned Himself. But because He was completely innocent, the spotless Lamb, death could not hold Him! His shed blood was without sin! Because Jesus was without sin and therefore death had no hold on Him, God had the right and even the obligation to raise Him from the dead.

Resurrection Life Saves You

The cross was no disaster! The cross was the place where God, through the death of His Son, made a way for us to come back into His presence and obtain eternal life again. And the resurrection proved it.

The Spirit of Life

But what does it say? "The word is near you, in your mouth and in your heart"(that is, the word of faith which we preach): that if you confess with your mouth the Lord Jesus and believe in your heart that God has raised Him from the dead, you will be saved. For with the heart one believes unto righteousness, and with the mouth confession is made unto salvation.

Romans 10:8-10

We call this a piece of the Roman Road because the Holy Spirit reveals our road to salvation in the book of Romans. We believe in our hearts that Jesus is alive, that He is raised from the dead, and confess openly that He is our Lord. That is the way we are saved. And that word "saved" means we are made completely whole spiritually, mentally, emotionally, and physically. We have been delivered from death into resurrection life.

The world will often call us "those born-agains," as though we made all this up. But it was Jesus who called salvation being born again, when He tried to explain salvation to a Jewish leader named Nicodemus.

There was a man of the Pharisees named Nicodemus, a ruler of the Jews. This man came to Jesus by night and said to Him, "Rabbi, we know that You are a teacher come from God; for no one can do these signs that You do unless God is with him."

Jesus answered and said to him, "Most assuredly, I say to you, unless one is born again, he cannot see the kingdom of God."

Resurrection Life Now!

Nicodemus said to Him, "How can a man be born when he is old? Can he enter a second time into his mother's womb and be born?"

Jesus answered, "Most assuredly, I say to you, unless one is born of water and the Spirit, he cannot enter the kingdom of God. That which is born of the flesh is flesh, and that which is born of the Spirit is spirit. Do not marvel that I said to you, 'You must be born again.' The wind blows where it wishes, and you hear the sound of it, but cannot tell where it comes from and where it goes. So is everyone who is born of the Spirit."

John 3:1-8

Jesus made it clear that no one is going to see or enter the kingdom of God without being born again. Like Nicodemus, some of us have a hard time understanding what being born again actually is, but we can understand a couple of things. First, it is spiritual not physical. And second, the Holy Spirit does it. We are "born of the Spirit." That's why Paul wrote in Romans 8:9, "Now if anyone does not have the Spirit of Christ, he is not His." Without the Spirit of God living on the inside of us, we are not born again, and we are not God's children.

How would you know if the Spirit of God dwells in you? Because you've believed God raised Jesus from the dead and you have told people that He is your Lord and Savior (Romans 10:9-10). The Bible says that when you do that, you are "born of the Spirit." I'll just tell you the truth. There are times you don't feel like the Spirit of the Living God is inside you, and there are other times when His presence is so real and wonderful that you just know anything is possible. But regardless of how you feel, He is there, filling you with His resurrection life.

In the beginning of this chapter I talked about the Buddhist monks praying to a dead, powerless god. They believed their prayers were acceptable and would be answered if they felt good when they prayed. But having the Spirit of God inside you isn't about how you feel; it's about what you know to be true by the Word of God.

Unbelievers feel and experience certain things in a supernatural way and think they are being spiritual. They say there are many ways into the spiritual realm. There are many doors. But we know what Jesus said:

> *Then Jesus said to them again, "Most assuredly, I say to you, I am the door of the sheep. All who ever came before Me are thieves and robbers, but the sheep did not hear them. I am the door. If anyone enters by Me, he will be saved, and will go in and out and find pasture. The thief does not come except to steal, and to kill, and to destroy. I have come that they may have life, and that they may have it more abundantly."*
>
> *John 10:7-10*

There are many dead gods—some are people who have died like Buddha and others are evil spirits like Allah—but there is only one Living Way. Jesus is the only door to true salvation and spiritual life, resurrection life, because He is the only one who has died and then been resurrected.

People try to get into the spiritual realm other ways. Some smoke weed. Some go to séances. Some play with Ouija boards. Some read Tarot cards and study their horoscopes. The world wants to know what's going to happen. They want to see into the future. They want knowledge and truth, but they don't want to know the God of all knowledge and truth, who knew the future from before the foundation of the world. They don't want to know Jesus, who is wisdom personified, who can give them abundant, resurrection life. But those who are in the flesh cannot please God.

Resurrection Life Now!

But you are not in the flesh but in the Spirit, if indeed the Spirit of God dwells in you. Now if anyone does not have the Spirit of Christ, he is not His.

Romans 8:8-9

To be honest, this last verse has always bothered me. I think about it a lot. I believe it, and I know it's right and true, but my heart sinks to even consider that there are people in this world who do not want to be born of the Spirit, who do not want to live the resurrection life Jesus gave His life to offer them. That's why I preach with all my heart. It's why I continue to pastor a church. I want to bring this great Gospel of the Lord Jesus Christ to as many people as I can, so they can be born again of the Spirit of God and have resurrection life.

Romans 8:9 says that if you do not have the Spirit of life, you do not know God. You are not His child. You are not one with Him. Being saved is about having the Spirit of life inside you, and when you have the Spirit of life inside, you have both eternal life and resurrection life.

Eternal Life and Resurrection Life

Noah Webster's 1828 dictionary defines "eternal" as:

Without beginning or end of existence.... everlasting; endless; immortal.... Perpetual; ceaseless; continued without intermission.... Unchangeable; existing at all times without change.... An appellation of God.

Eternal is forever and for all time, which means you are dealing with God. He's forever. So eternal life is both a quantity and quality of life. When we have eternal life, we will live forever (quantity) and we will live with God, who is life, love, joy, and peace (quality). Resurrection life is the manifestation of eternal life in our lives right now.

Resurrection Life Saves You

Resurrection simply means "to rise." Noah Webster defines it as, "a rising again." Resurrection life revives you and lifts you up. It's the kind of life that can even overcome death in your mortal body, but it's even more than that. Jesus was resurrected, and that means all those who believe He was resurrected from the dead have His resurrection life.

We received eternal life the moment we believed God raised Jesus from the dead and confessed Jesus as our Lord. We know this because just before Jesus raised Lazarus from the dead, He told Lazarus' sister Martha,

"I am the resurrection and the life. He who believes in Me, though he may die, he shall live. And whoever lives and believes in Me shall never die."

John 11:25-26

Jesus said, "I Am the rising-from-the-dead kind of life." Not only do we have eternal life, where we will live forever with the Lord, but we also have the kind of life that lifts us, raises us up, and causes us to be victorious over anything that would hold us down, keep us under, pull us back, hinder us, or stop us altogether in our present life on earth.

Are you getting this?

Now think about it. I'm talking differently about resurrection life. This is not like Easter. I'm not talking about resurrection morning when Jesus rose from the dead, although that's the foundation of it. Nor am I talking about the end times, when our bodies will be resurrected into immortal bodies. The resurrection life I'm talking about is in you right now.

But if the Spirit of Him who raised Jesus from the dead dwells in you, He who raised Christ from the dead will also give life to your mortal bodies through His Spirit who dwells in you.

Romans 8:11

Resurrection Life Now!

Resurrection life comes from the Holy Spirit inside you. He is the Spirit of resurrection life. The Holy Spirit is there to raise you up, to lift you, and to empower you in every challenge of life—just like He did Jesus. Romans 8:9 says, "But you are not in the flesh but in the Spirit, if indeed the Spirit of God dwells in you." When you were saved you became a living spirit, alive through the Spirit of God. You are no longer just a body with a mind, emotions, and will. You are a spiritual child of the Living God, and you live from your spirit instead of your soul. Your spirit is no longer dead and separated from the eternal life of God, so you can now live according to the resurrection life you have in Christ Jesus.

People who are not born again are still bound in their flesh because their spirits are dead to God. The Holy Spirit is not in them, so they don't have spiritual life. Did you ever try to interview a dead person? A person without God does not perceive God. They don't see Him, hear Him, discern Him, feel Him, or know Him. Some spiritually dead people don't even believe there is a God or don't want to know if there is a God. They are spiritually disconnected from the eternal life of God, and they have no way of understanding how a believer walks in the resurrection life of God.

The Bible tells us that before we were born again into the eternal and resurrection life of God by the Spirit of life, we were dead. The Holy Spirit uses that word "dead."

And you He made alive, who were dead in trespasses and sins.

Ephesians 2:1

"Most assuredly, I say to you, he who hears My word and believes in Him who sent Me has everlasting life, and shall not come into judgment, but has passed from death into life."

John 5:24

Resurrection Life Saves You

When we were born again, we passed from a living death to a res-urrection life. We now have eternal life, but we also have the Spirit of life on the inside of us, making all the dead things in our lives alive. We are alive because Jesus is alive! We are saved from death and damna-tion forever—and we are saved from death and damnation today as we walk in His resurrection life now!

Resurrection Life Now!

Chapter 3

Resurrection Life Restores You

Sometimes God shows me something that is mind-boggling. It's overwhelming because it makes so much sense. It is reasonable in God's way of thinking and doing things; and really, as His child I realize that my mind is finally comprehending what I already knew in my spirit. That's why I rejoice and know it is absolutely true from the core of my being.

What I'm talking about is the astounding restoration that takes place when the resurrection life of the Holy Spirit comes to live inside us and we become a new creation in Christ Jesus. When we are saved, we are restored to God! Spiritually, we return to Him and enjoy His presence. We can walk and talk with our Heavenly Father, with our Lord Jesus Christ, and receive comfort, instruction, and guidance from the Holy Spirit. The Word of God is no longer a dead letter but miraculous and alive, and the words of our Heavenly Father and our Lord Jesus Christ jump off the page into our hearts by the power of the Holy Spirit. We have God's resurrection life inside us, intimately joining us to Him forever. We have holy communion with the Creator of the Universe, and He's our Abba, Father!

Resurrection Life Now!

Jesus' Prayer for You

Jesus spoke these words, lifted up His eyes to heaven, and said:

"Father, the hour has come. Glorify Your Son, that Your Son also may glorify You, as You have given Him authority over all flesh, that He should give eternal life to as many as You have given Him. And this is eternal life, that they may know You, the only true God, and Jesus Christ whom You have sent.

John 17:1-3

Jesus gave us another definition of eternal life: knowing God. Let's look at the next section of this prayer:

"I have glorified You on the earth. I have finished the work which You have given Me to do. And now, O Father, glorify Me together with Yourself, with the glory which I had with You before the world was."

John 17:4-5

Jesus had become a human being and was about to endure death on the cross, and yet He said, "I have finished the work which You have given Me to do." But He hadn't gone to the cross! He hadn't been resurrected, so how could He say that?

If you remember the first chapter of this book, you will understand how He could say that: He was slain from before the foundation of the world. To Jesus, the cross was a done deal! In verse 5 He said, "Oh Father, glorify Me together with Yourself, with the glory which I had with You before the world was." As He prayed, His death and resurrection were before that time and were before Him then. And because they were before Him, there was no doubt in His mind and heart that they would be accomplished. He was there to do the will of His Father.

Resurrection Life Restores You

"I have manifested Your name to the men whom You have given Me out of the world. They were Yours, You gave them to Me, and they have kept Your word. Now they have known that all things which You have given Me are from You. For I have given to them the words which You have given Me; and they have received them, and have known surely that I came forth from You; and they have believed that You sent Me.

"I pray for them. I do not pray for the world but for those whom You have given Me, for they are Yours. And all Mine are Yours, and Yours are Mine, and I am glorified in them. Now I am no longer in the world, but these are in the world, and I come to You. Holy Father, keep through Your name those whom You have given Me, that they may be one as We are."

John 17:6-11

Jesus asked the Father to watch over us and protect us while we are in this world, and then for the first time He said, "...that they may be one as We are." He said that we are both His and the Father's, that He is glorified in us, and we can be one with Him and the Father just as He and the Father are one. Are you getting this?

In verse 20 Jesus says, "I do not pray for these alone, but also for those who will believe in Me through their word." He's talking about you and me!

"I do not pray for these alone, but also for those who will believe in Me through their word; that they all may be one, as You, Father, are in Me, and I in You; that they also may be one in Us, that the world may believe that You sent Me. And the glory which You gave Me I have given them, that they may be one just as We are one: I in them, and You in Me; that they may be made

perfect in one, and that the world may know that You have sent Me, and have loved them as You have loved Me.

"Father, I desire that they also whom You gave Me may be with Me where I am, that they may behold My glory which You have given Me; for You loved Me before the foundation of the world. O righteous Father! The world has not known You, but I have known You; and these have known that You sent Me. And I have declared to them Your name, and will declare it, that the love with which You loved Me may be in them, and I in them."

John 17:20-26

Jesus and the Father had an agreement that Jesus would become a human being and die on the cross for the sins of all mankind. He would be the spotless, innocent Lamb, whose sinless blood would pay the debt we owed to God for our sin. Why would God the Father and Jesus the Son want to do this? What was worth everything that the Son gave up to become a human being? What was the joy He looked forward to as He endured the rejection, the beatings, the whipping, and the cross? It was the restoration of our relationship with the Godhead!

What We Lost Through Adam

Adam was created in the image of God. He had a flesh and bone body, and he had a soul with a mind, emotions, and will. But he was primarily a spirit being like his Creator. Jesus told the woman at the well, "God is Spirit, and those who worship Him must worship in spirit and truth" (John 4:24). And Genesis 3:8 reveals that God walked in the Garden of Eden with Adam and Eve. They communicated spirit to spirit. They walked and talked together as spirit beings, and I don't think they spoke in Hebrew, Latin, or Greek. They spoke God's language of the Spirit.

Resurrection Life Restores You

Adam and Eve were one with the Father, the Son, and the Holy Spirit. They communicated with all three freely. God shared His mind and heart with them. He told them why He created them and what He wanted them to accomplish on the earth. He gave them dominion over it and commanded them to be fruitful and multiply; and He blessed them (Genesis 1:26-28). He showed them the beautiful, perfect garden He had created just for them and commanded them to tend it and guard it. This was the special place on earth where He would walk and talk with them.

Genesis 1:31 reveals that God created Adam on the sixth day, and Genesis 2:2 says that on the seventh day He rested. This doesn't mean He went to bed and slept or sat down and watched TV. He spent the entire first day of Adam's life with Adam! With God, rest has always meant intimacy and communion with Him. As human beings, we were created to find rest only in the presence of God. That's why we can be in the midst of the greatest battle or storm and rest in God. We can rest in Him continually.

Today, if we wanted to describe God's day of rest on that seventh day, we would say that He and Adam just hung out together. There was no naming of animals or tending the garden; it was just the two of them walking and talking, sitting together, sharing their hearts and minds with one another like a father with a beloved son or daughter.

One of the things God shared with Adam when He put him in the Garden was this:

And the LORD God commanded the man, saying, "Of every tree of the garden you may freely eat; but of the tree of the knowledge of good and evil you shall not eat, for in the day that you eat of it you shall surely die."

Genesis 2:16-17

Resurrection Life Now!

In the original Hebrew language, "surely die" is actually "die die." The words "surely" and "die" are the same Hebrew word *muwth*, which means to die.[1] God actually said to Adam (my paraphrase), "If you eat of the tree of the knowledge of good and evil, you will die twice." What was He talking about? How can anyone die twice?

We know that the moment Adam and Eve ate of the tree of the knowledge of good and evil, they didn't die physically. That took a long time. But when they ate that forbidden fruit, they changed drastically. When God came looking for them in Genesis 3:8, they hid from Him. They were afraid to be in His presence. This is a far cry from freely walking and talking with God, like they had always done before. Why would they be afraid of Him? He had done nothing but love them and bless them.

When they ate of that tree and disobeyed the word of the Lord, they immediately died spiritually. Their spirits were severed from the life and presence of God forever. They lost eternal life, which can only come from Him. Then, because the eternal, spiritual life of God had left them, their physical bodies began to die.

After the Fall, there was no eternal life in Adam and Eve, no Holy Spirit to sustain them physically, mentally, or emotionally. Their souls became afraid and ashamed, causing them to hide from the God of faith and righteousness. Their bodies were suddenly filled with death instead of eternal life, causing them to begin the process of decay and making them susceptible to disease. Being spiritually dead was terrible!

Adam and Eve were dead spiritually, so they had no way of communicating with God spirit to spirit. They could only communicate with Him through their soul and physical senses. The first couple (and therefore all human beings descended from them) no longer were the spiritual people they were created to be. They were lost and undone because they had lost the most important thing: their intimate communion with God as spiritual beings.

The Life-Giving Spirit

There is a natural body, and there is a spiritual body. And so it is written, "The first man Adam became a living being." The last Adam became a life-giving spirit. However, the spiritual is not first, but the natural, and afterward the spiritual.

1 Corinthians 15:44-46

If Adam had lived in our time, after the Fall he would have said, "Houston, we have a problem." That problem was spiritual death. We were separated from the life of God because of our sin. We needed to be spiritually rejoined to the Father. Somehow, our sin needed to be removed and blotted out so that our spirits could be reunited with God's Spirit. Thank God, He had a plan in place from before the foundation of the world.

Now I want to make this clear: Even spiritually dead, Adam and Eve were not beyond the love and grace of God. They knew they could call on Him, but they called on Him in a different way. First Corinthians 15:45 NASB says that Adam literally became (after the Fall) a living soul. It didn't say he was still a spirit with a soul, because his spirit was dead. Adam and Eve and the entire human race now lived according to their mind, emotions, will, and physical senses instead of their spirits in communion with the Holy Spirit. And so they communicated with God in the physical realm, not the spiritual realm.

Throughout history, people have reached and looked for God. In fact, they have come up with all kinds of ideas about how to be restored to Him and reconnected with Him. But God always had the better plan.

Resurrection Life Now!

God, who at various times and in various ways spoke in time past to the fathers by the prophets, has in these last days spoken to us by His Son, whom He has appointed heir of all things, through whom also He made the worlds; who being the brightness of His glory and the express image of His person, and upholding all things by the word of His power, when He had by Himself purged our sins, sat down at the right hand of the Majesty on high, having become so much better than the angels, as He has by inheritance obtained a more excellent name than they.

Hebrews 1:1-4

God sent Jesus to speak to us. He was the second and last Adam. The first Adam began a spiritually dead, sinful human race, and the last Adam would bring forth a restored, righteous human race. God called Jesus the last Adam because He was our last chance to be restored! This last Adam would also bring forth a race of human beings, and God ordained that there would never be another one. But this race of human beings would be living spirits, not just living souls.

Through His death and resurrection, the last Adam, the Lord Jesus Christ, became a life-giving spirit. Through Him, our spirits could be "born again" and rejoined to the Father through the indwelling of the Holy Spirit. When we are "born from above" we cease to be mere humans in a robe of clay, living from our physical senses, natural reasoning, and feelings. We are spiritually reunited with our Father God, can communicate with Him spirit to spirit, and have His ability—His resurrection life—to reject sin and live holy, consecrated lives.

Jesus is a life-giving Spirit, who imparts both eternal life and resurrection life to us when we are born again. We will live forever with God in eternity, intimately joined to Him spiritually; but we also have the same Spirit that raised Jesus from the dead living in us—whose function is to continually bring alive all the dead things in our lives while we live on earth. Jesus, the last Adam, gives us resurrection life for right now.

You Are Consubstantial with God

A person can be a senator, a teacher, a homemaker, or a truck driver without God. People on this earth can do amazing things without God. But they are merely living souls. They have no eternal or resurrection life in them, so they do not freely communicate with God or get to know Him intimately. They cannot hear the voice of the Holy Spirit inside them because He is not there. As a result, they will miss God's love, blessing, and plan for their lives. They will not understand His Word. The Holy Bible will be a dead letter to them because God's words are spirit and are spiritually understood. All this because they are spiritually dead.

> It is the Spirit who gives life; the flesh profits nothing. The words that I speak to you are spirit, and they are life.
>
> *John 6:63*

> Now we have received, not the spirit of the world, but the Spirit who is from God, that we might know the things that have been freely given to us by God. These things we also speak, not in words which man's wisdom teaches but which the Holy Spirit teaches, comparing spiritual things with spiritual. But the natural man does not receive the things of the Spirit of God, for they are foolishness to him; nor can he know them, because they are spiritually discerned.
>
> *1 Corinthians 2:12-14*

Resurrection Life Now!

People just exist without God, but when they hear the Good News, the Gospel of Jesus Christ, submit to the convicting power of the Holy Spirit that they are sinners in need of a Savior, and receive Jesus as that Savior, they become spiritually alive to God. They become His child.

We talk about that all the time, but what does it really mean to be a child of God? When I was conceived and then born physically, I was given my parents' DNA or genetic make-up. I inherited certain physical looks, mannerisms, strengths, and weaknesses from my parents. I also inherited personality traits, gifts, and talents from them. That's my physical DNA.

When I got born again spiritually, literally born from above, I was given God's spiritual DNA. The Bible says I have His love, joy, peace, longsuffering, kindness, goodness, faithfulness, gentleness, and self-control in me. (Galatians 5:22)

For He made Him who knew no sin to be sin for us, that we might become the righteousness of God in Him.

2 Corinthians 5:21

In my spirit, I am righteous like Jesus is. I now have the ability to be and act just like Jesus.

But he who is joined to the Lord is one spirit with Him.

1 Corinthians 6:17

This is what Jesus was praying about in John, chapter 17. He was talking about us being one with God through our spirits. If you have been born again, something magnificent has happened in you. God has connected you to Himself as His spirit child. He has imparted to you His spiritual DNA, and you are reunited and plugged into His Spirit and His Truth. No wonder the Bible says in 1 John 4:4, "He who is in you is greater than he who is in the world"!

Resurrection Life Restores You

I learned a new word that perfectly describes this oneness Jesus spoke about in John 17—consubstantial. According to Webster, means, "Having the same substance or essence ... of the same kind or nature."

The first Adam was consubstantial with God until he ate of the tree of the knowledge of good and evil. When he went his own way, Adam gave up the condition—the eternal spiritual condition—of being consubstantial with God. Then Jesus, the last Adam, came to Earth as fully human as well as being spiritually consubstantial with God. His spirit was in continuous contact with God even though He lived in a robe of clay.

When you received the eternal life offered by Jesus, who is the life-giving Spirit, you became spiritually consubstantial with Him and God. You are no longer just human flesh that will die and live forever in Hell, separated from the presence of your Creator forever. No! You have God's DNA. You are made of His spiritual substance and essence. You are of His kind and have His nature. You are consubstantial with the Living God!

What Difference Does It Make?

Now that you are restored to the Father through the blood of Jesus Christ, now that you have His DNA, His substance, His essence, His character, and His power, how should that effect your life?

And the glory which You gave Me I have given them, that they may be one just as We are one: I in them, and You in Me; that they may be made perfect in one.

John 17:22-23

You are to be made perfect in this new spiritual condition of being consubstantial and one with God. The word "perfect" literally means to become complete.[2] In another translation, Jesus said,

Resurrection Life Now!

*I in them and you in me, in order that they, having been brought
to the state of completeness with respect to oneness, may persist
in that state of completeness.*

John 17:22-23 WUEST

Jesus is talking about spiritual maturity. When you were born
again, you were brought into "the state of completeness with respect to
oneness," but Jesus went on to pray that you "may persist in that state
of completeness." You are to grow up and mature in Him. The Spirit
who lives in you is in the business of bringing you to maturity; His job
is to bring the Church to maturity. You mature when you live from the
resurrection life of the Holy Spirit inside you.

All of us must continually advance in the knowledge of God and
the revelation of His Word. We must persist in this. It troubles me
when people say things like,

- "I go to church because I love the music."

- "I go to church because that's where my friends go."

- "I go to church because it is fun."

All those things are wonderful, and I hope you do have wonderful
friends, love the music, and have fun. Furthermore, if that's what is
getting you to church, then keep going! But Beloved, you need to make
sure you are born again and have been restored to the Father, that you
and He are one. And once you are certain of that, you need to grow
spiritually, to persist in your newfound completeness with God.

Having the resurrection life of God on the inside of you makes an
incredible difference in your life for many reasons, but the main one
is that you have been restored to the Father. You can hear His voice on
the inside of you. You can walk and talk with Him just like Adam and

Resurrection Life Restores You

Eve did, and just like Jesus did when He walked this earth. You are now a living spirit, and your spirit is connected to God by the Holy Spirit inside you.

> *For as many as are led by the Spirit of God, these are sons of God.*

> *Romans 8:14*

You are not led by the government, the evening news, or the latest fashions and trends of society. You are led by the Spirit of God. You are full of grace and truth because you are in Christ, and He is full of grace and truth (John 1:14). You are consubstantial with your Father, so you have His nature—but you must partake of it.

> *... have been given to us exceedingly great and precious promises, that through these you may be partakers of the divine nature.*

> *2 Peter 1:4*

I want you to zero in on "you may be partakers of the divine nature." Adam lost the divine nature when he ate of the tree of the knowledge of good and evil, but through the Lord Jesus Christ, God's divine nature was restored to you and you can grow in it every day as you read, study, and meditate on His "exceedingly great and precious promises." Hallelujah!

The resurrection life inside you restores you to God so you can partake of His divine nature. You can walk and talk with Him. It doesn't matter where you are or what you are doing, He is there and you can rest in His presence, draw on His strength, search out His wisdom on a matter, and even have a good laugh with Him. You can go to your own "garden" to pray, to listen, to just wait on Him to speak. And you can open your heart and mind to see and hear more and more revelation as you read and study His Word.

Resurrection Life Now!

But God, who is rich in mercy, because of His great love with which He loved us, even when we were dead in trespasses, made us alive together with Christ (by grace you have been saved), and raised us up together, and made us sit together in the heavenly places in Christ Jesus.

Ephesians 2:4-6

Do you realize that at any moment of time in your life, you can sit with your Father in Heaven, right beside Jesus, and rise above the trials and horrors of this world to get a divine understanding and perspective on your life and what is happening around you? You can live from a higher place! This is where God reveals His plans and purposes for you. It is where He gives you joy and courage to meet all the challenges of your life. And it is where you move from discouragement and defeat to confidence and victory.

Resurrection life restores you to God, and what difference does it make? Beyond your imagination!

Chapter 4

Resurrection Life Endues You

You're more than you think you are.

You are capable of so much more than the world, the devil, or your carnal thinking will tell you! Honestly, I've been a Christian for a long, long time, and sometimes I wonder if, instead of reading the Bible, the children of God are reading *Christianity for Dummies,* because we act like we don't know who we are or what we have in Christ Jesus.

If you really are a dummy, then God your Father has to be the big dummy, and you know that's a lie. Your Father is the Creator of the Universe, the compassionate, loving God who possesses all wisdom and power. If you are His son or daughter, you are no dummy! You are not helpless and hopeless. You are supernaturally able to overcome sin, the world, and the enemy while doing great exploits.

How easily we forget the truth about who we are in Christ and what God promises us in His Word. We forget about it, or we have so little Word in us that we don't have the faith to pray and believe we can have what He says we can have. As a result, we believe only the pastor or the healing evangelist can preach and get supernatural results. I hope you are beginning to see that this is just not true. Why? Because you are living and walking in resurrection life now!

- You were foreordained to walk in the works God has predestined you to walk in—in His resurrection life.

- You have been saved from sin, eternal damnation, and darkness, and all dead things in your life are made alive—in His resurrection life.

- You have been restored to fellowship and intimate communion with God—in His resurrection life.

Now it is time for you to understand that you are endued with power in your resurrection life. Believers refer to this experience in many ways, and each way can be found in the various translations of the Bible. Some will call it "the infilling of the Holy Spirit" or "being filled with the Holy Spirit." Jesus called it "the gift of the Holy Spirit" and being "endued with power from on high." Many call this "the baptism in the Holy Spirit," so let's begin by understanding what baptism is.

The Powerful Symbolism of Water Baptism

"Go therefore and make disciples of all the nations, baptizing them in the name of the Father and of the Son and of the Holy Spirit."

Matthew 28:19

To comprehend the amazing experience of being baptized in the Holy Spirit, let's talk about being water baptized. This is something most Christians can relate to. The word "baptized" means to be repeatedly immersed and submerged.[1] Some denominations sprinkle people with water, but to really identify with the death, burial, and resurrection of the Lord Jesus Christ, we need to be immersed in water. The water symbolizes the grave, but it also represents the washing of the water of the Word of God and the power of the Holy Spirit to make us brand-new.

Resurrection Life Endues You

Now think about this: In water baptism, we don't immerse ourselves. Our pastor or another believer immerses us. This lets us know that we can't save ourselves. God saves us. We give our lives to Him and the Holy Spirit turns our dead spirit into a live spirit and comes to live in us forever. Again, we cannot save ourselves, but God is pleased to save us, to raise us up, and to give us eternal life and resurrection life.

We are submerged in the water to identify with the death and burial of Jesus, then we are brought up out of the water to identify with His resurrection. We go down dry sinners and we come up out of that water as spiritually alive saints of God, baptized in resurrection life. Water baptism physically demonstrates what happens to us when we are born again spiritually.

> Or do you not know that as many of us as were baptized into Christ Jesus were baptized into His death? Therefore we were buried with Him through baptism into death, that just as Christ was raised from the dead by the glory of the Father, even so we also should walk in newness of life.
>
> For if we have been united together in the likeness of His death, certainly we also shall be in the likeness of His resurrection.
>
> Romans 6:3-5

Some Christians don't understand how precious water baptism is, either because they have never done it or they don't know they should do it. They need to read Matthew 28:19, where Jesus commanded us to be water baptized after we are born again. In fact, it is one of the two sacraments of the Church He told us to always practice: water baptism and communion (where we symbolically partake of His body and blood to remind us of the powerful covenant we entered into when we were born again).

Resurrection Life Now!

We know Peter remembered what Jesus had said. After he preached the first Gospel sermon on the Day of Pentecost, many were cut to the heart and cried out, "What must we do to be saved?" This is what Peter answered:

> *"Repent, and let every one of you be baptized in the name of Jesus Christ for the remission of sins; and you shall receive the gift of the Holy Spirit. For the promise is to you and to your children, and to all who are afar off, as many as the Lord our God will call."*
>
> *Acts 2:38-39*

Everyone Is to be Baptized in Water!

I want you to notice something else Peter told the people on the Day of Pentecost. He said they would receive the gift of the Holy Spirit. He also said that this was not only for the people who were listening to him that day, but it was also for "all who are afar off, as many as the Lord our God will call." Peter was talking about you and me!

Now before I go on, I must address a problem that has arisen in some denominations regarding water baptism. Some believe and teach that if someone is not water baptized they will go to Hell, regardless of whether they have been born again. However, the thief on the cross believed in Jesus, and Jesus told him that he would see him in Paradise (Luke 23:43). Furthermore, in Romans 2:28-29 Paul says that salvation is spiritual not physical, of the heart and not the flesh. In Ephesians, Paul explains that our works, including water baptism, are not what saves us:

> *For by grace you have been saved through faith, and that not of yourselves; it is the gift of God, not of works, lest anyone should boast.*
>
> *Ephesians 2:8-9*

Resurrection Life Endues You

If your daddy got saved on his deathbed and couldn't be water baptized, be assured by the Word of God that he is in Heaven with Jesus. It is unfortunate that he couldn't enjoy the amazing experience of being baptized in water, to know more deeply the miracle of being born again and now a part of God's family, but the important thing is that he is in Heaven and is discovering and learning in the presence of His Lord and Savior.

As for us, we can still know the joy of water baptism, which illustrates to us in a very tangible way what happens to us when we receive the gift of the Holy Spirit Jesus commanded us to receive.

The Gift of the Holy Spirit

Outside of receiving the Lord Jesus Christ as my personal Savior, I have never in my life received anything more powerful, more life-changing, and more dynamic than when I received the gift of the Holy Spirit. This happened when I was sixteen and attended a little tent meeting in Corpus Christi, Texas. A woman named Freda Lindsay spoke on being filled with the Holy Spirit. (Later, she and her husband Gordon founded Christ for the Nations in Dallas, Texas, which is still one of America's most wonderful Bible and ministry training schools.)

I went to this meeting because I had heard they prayed for the sick. I did not go to be filled with the Holy Spirit, but I was soon to discover that God had much more for me. As Mrs. Lindsay ministered on the Holy Spirit, it was so real to me. What she said struck a chord deep in my heart. Then she said, "Everyone who wants to receive the Holy Spirit, stand up." My body stood up, but my mind was still sitting down. I didn't tell my body to get up, and I wanted to sit down; but I was afraid if I moved, somebody would notice me and I'd be embarrassed.

Resurrection Life Now!

People who have known me since that time cannot believe how shy and timid I was. I was completely self-conscious. But somehow the Holy Spirit got me to stand up so He could have permission to fill me up—and boy, did He fill me! I was not partially filled. I didn't get a little bit. I got a whole lot of the Holy Spirit. The third person of the Godhead exploded in my earthen vessel, and I was completely immersed in power from on high. I have never been the same since! The fire in my belly has never subsided.

Many years later, a pastor where I was ministering said, "Sister Anne gets really excited about the power of the Holy Spirit." He said it like it was some new phenomenon to me, so when I spoke, I gently corrected him by saying that I was the most timid girl in Texas until I was baptized in the Holy Ghost sixteen years before, and yes, I had been excited and bold as a lion ever since!

Before we go any deeper into the discussion of the gift of the Holy Spirit, I want to take a look at the Holy Spirit as the third person of the Godhead. Obviously, He is a spirit. He does not have a physical form like Jesus. He is a spirit being like God the Father. He is called the Holy Spirit, which means there is only one. And believe me, He is the only spirit you want living inside you! Then, notice that the adjective used to describe Him is "holy." Here is one of the most thorough definitions of the Greek word *hagios*, translated holy: "Set apart, sanctified, consecrated, saint. It has a common root … with … chaste, pure. Its fundamental idea is separation, consecration, devotion to the service of Deity, sharing in God's purity and abstaining from earth's defilement."[2]

The Spirit of God is called holy because He is fully devoted to serving God the Father and God the Son (His function) and He is pure and undefiled (His nature). He is a sacred spirit, as sacred as the Father and the Son, and He is equal with the Father and the Son. So we need to have the same reverence and respect for Him as we do Jesus and our Heavenly Father.

The next thing you need to know about the Holy Spirit is that He is absolutely necessary to your salvation and your walk with God. Just before He ascended to the Father, Jesus told His disciples not to go anywhere or to do anything without the gift of the Holy Spirit:

And being assembled together with them, He commanded them not to depart from Jerusalem, but to wait for the Promise of the Father, "which," He said, "you have heard from Me; for John truly baptized with water, but you shall be baptized with the Holy Spirit not many days from now...."

Acts 1:4-5

Jesus mentioned John the Baptist, probably because John had told his followers about Jesus and what He would do.

"I indeed baptize you with water unto repentance, but He who is coming after me is mightier than I, whose sandals I am not worthy to carry. He will baptize you with the Holy Spirit and fire."

Matthew 3:11

This verse tells us that Jesus is the one who baptizes us into the resurrection life and power of the Holy Spirit. I want you to notice that John's baptism of repentance in water came first. Repentance means to turn, to change your mind, to simply stop living for yourself and begin living for God. John the Baptist immersed people in water to symbolize a cleansing from sin, and all sin comes from serving yourself instead of God. So when they were baptized, those people went down into the water self-serving and came out of the water to love and serve God alone.

Resurrection Life Now!

This is important symbolically because many people want to move in the power of the Holy Spirit without cleaning up their lives. They want to go to Heaven, cast out devils, heal the sick, preach and prophesy, but they don't want to deal with the areas of sin that are plaguing them. This is why we need to reverence ALL the work of the Holy Spirit and remember that His name is not the Power Spirit; His name is the Holy Spirit. God is just as interested in the condition of our souls as He is interested in what we do for Him. In fact, if we don't allow Him to clean up our lives, eventually our sins will overtake us and destroy any ministry we have, no matter how powerful it is.

Now that we understand how important it is to remain humble and repentant, those who are born again, whose whole hearts are turned toward serving the Lord, should certainly ask Jesus to baptize them to receive the gift of the Holy Spirit.

The Holy Spirit and Fire

What did John the Baptist mean when he said Jesus would baptize you in fire? Some teachers will tell you that it means judgment, that Jesus will judge your life, and the conviction of the Holy Spirit will be so intense that you will feel like Jesus is literally burning the sin out of your life. Christians will say, "God's got me in the fire right now. I'm being purged and pruned."

I believe it can be hard and even painful to overcome areas of sin in our lives, and you can feel like you are literally going through fire; but I don't believe that this was the "fire" John the Baptist was seeing. As a prophet, standing on the banks of the Jordan River and watching Jesus approach, I believe John saw Jesus in the future. What he saw in the spirit caused him to say that Jesus would baptize believers in the Holy Spirit and fire. John saw the saints in the Upper Room, being baptized in the Holy Spirit, with fire on their heads.

Resurrection Life Endues You

To me that fire speaks of the glory, the same glory that shone from Moses' face so brightly that the people begged him to put a veil over his head. He had been in the presence of God for so many days that when he came down the mountain, his face shone with the glory of God. (See Exodus 34:29-35.) That happened under the Old Covenant, when God said that no man could look upon Him and live. When the saints came under the New Covenant in Jesus' blood, filled with His resurrection life on the Day of Pentecost, the glory on them looked like tongues of fire.

> When the Day of Pentecost had fully come, they were all with one accord in one place. And suddenly there came a sound from heaven, as of a rushing mighty wind, and it filled the whole house where they were sitting. Then there appeared to them divided tongues, as of fire, and one sat upon each of them. And they were all filled with the Holy Spirit and began to speak with other tongues, as the Spirit gave them utterance.
>
> *Acts 2:1-4*

When Jesus baptizes us in the Holy Spirit, dynamic things start happening!

I have already told you about my experience, and how being filled with the Holy Spirit transformed me from a shy, timid girl into a bold witness for the Lord Jesus Christ. The way I have always expressed this is that I have a fire in my belly.

We see the same thing happen to the saints in the Upper Room. Remember, Jesus had just been crucified, and a lot of religious people were extremely angry that some Jews were saying Jesus had risen from the dead and the tomb was empty. That's why His disciples were laying low and hiding out. They were frightened about what might happen to them if they were identified as disciples of Jesus of Nazareth.

Resurrection Life Now!

Somehow, 120 of them managed to gather in that Upper Room. And they waited. They had no clue what they were waiting for. They weren't waiting to make a demonstration. They weren't waiting to speak with other tongues or to preach the Gospel. They simply were waiting for what Jesus said He wanted them to have. He had told them:

"But you shall receive power when the Holy Spirit has come upon you; and you shall be witnesses to Me in Jerusalem, and in all Judea and Samaria, and to the end of the earth."

Acts 1:8

They waited. They prayed. They wondered.

And suddenly there came a sound from heaven, as of a rushing mighty wind, and it filled the whole house where they were sitting.

Acts 2:2

All of a sudden there came a sound that was not natural. It came from another dimension, from the spiritual realm of Heaven.

Then there appeared to them divided tongues, as of fire, and one sat upon each of them.

Acts 2:3

"Then there appeared." I love that! They saw something. First they heard the Holy Spirit, and then they saw the Holy Spirit. And I want you to notice that initially His fire came and sat on them. But then,

...they were all filled with the Holy Spirit and began to speak with other tongues, as the Spirit gave them utterance.

Acts 2:4

Resurrection Life Endues You

The Holy Spirit blew into the physical realm. His fire sat on them and then filled them. They were so filled with the fire of God in their bellies that their tongues could not be silent! And in that spiritual state, the Holy Spirit gave them utterance in languages that were not their own.

But something even more dramatic happened when that mighty, rushing wind blew into the Upper Room. They didn't only speak with other tongues and shine with the glory of God. They ran out into the streets and continued speaking in what turned out to be the languages of people from all over the ancient world (Acts 1:5-11). The very ones who were scared to death to have anyone notice them now made a public spectacle of themselves!

The crowd that formed was astounded but skeptical. Some made fun of the saints.

"We hear them speaking in our own tongues the wonderful works of God." So they were all amazed and perplexed, saying to one another, "Whatever could this mean?"

Others mocking said, "They are full of new wine."

Acts 1:11-13

The angry religious people had not changed, but the disciples certainly had! Remember how Peter had denied the Lord three times and run away after Jesus had been arrested (Luke 22:55-62)? Look what the baptism in the Holy Spirit did to him:

But Peter, standing up with the eleven, raised his voice and said to them, "Men of Judea and all who dwell in Jerusalem, let this be known to you, and heed my words. For these are not drunk, as you suppose, since it is only the third hour of the day. But this is what was spoken by the prophet Joel:

Resurrection Life Now!

'And it shall come to pass in the last days, says God, 'That I will pour out of My Spirit on all flesh.''

Acts 2:14-17

Peter proceeded to preach the first Gospel message, and here is some more of it:

"Men of Israel, hear these words: Jesus of Nazareth, a Man attested by God to you by miracles, wonders, and signs which God did through Him in your midst, as you yourselves also know — Him, being delivered by the determined purpose and foreknowledge of God, you have taken by lawless hands, have crucified, and put to death; whom God raised up, having loosed the pains of death, because it was not possible that He should be held by it.

Acts 2:22-24

Not only does Peter confirm that God has raised Jesus of Nazareth from the dead, but also he confronts the "Men of Israel"—the very ones he had hid from before the Day of Pentecost—with the fact that they had crucified their own Messiah. Like me and every other believer who has been truly baptized in the Holy Spirit, Peter was transformed from a scared rabbit into a roaring lion. From this day forward, he and the other disciples never stopped preaching the Gospel and doing the works Jesus had done—no matter how dangerous it was. Like me, they had a fresh fire in their bellies!

Are You Pickled?

Certainly, an incredible change took place in Peter and those disciples after they received the gift of the Holy Spirit. It was the opposite of what happened to Adam and Eve when they sinned against God. They became afraid and ashamed and hid from God. They could no longer communicate with Him in the heavenly language of the Spirit. On the other hand, when the disciples were baptized in the Holy Spirit, they ran out to proclaim Jesus to the world. No fear or shame! And they spoke from their spirits by the power of the Holy Spirit as a new human race of spiritual beings. They had been miraculously transformed!

When I was doing research on the word *baptizo*, I found the following note:

> Not to be confused with 911, *bapto*. The clearest example that shows the meaning of *baptizo* is a text from the Greek poet and physician Nicander, who lived about 200 B.C. It is a recipe for making pickles and is helpful because it uses both words. Nicander says that in order to make a pickle, the vegetable should first be 'dipped' (bapto) into boiling water and then 'baptised' (baptizo) in the vinegar solution. Both verbs concern the immersing of vegetables in a solution. But the first is temporary. The second, the act of baptising the vegetable, produces a permanent change. When used in the New Testament, this word more often refers to our union and identification with Christ than to our water baptism. e.g. Mark 16:16. 'He that believes and is baptised shall be saved.' Christ is saying that mere intellectual assent is not enough. There must be a union with him, a real change, like the vegetable to the pickle! Bible Study Magazine, James Montgomery Boice, May 1989.[3]

When the cucumber is dipped in boiling water, this cleans the outside. The water makes a difference on the outside of that cucumber, but it doesn't change the fundamental essence of the cucumber and make it a pickle. The cleansing and change is temporary. This would be like John the Baptist's baptism in water: a necessary experience but not permanently transforming.

Resurrection Life Now!

On the other hand, the vinegar solution is like Jesus' baptism in the Holy Spirit. After you clean the cucumber with water, you immerse it in a vinegar solution. The vinegar saturates the cucumber inside and out to transform it into a pickle, producing a permanent change inside and out.

A lot of people are dipped in water and never have been born again. They never really came to know, love, and serve God. They just got baptized in water, thinking that that physical cleansing would wash away their sins and make them holy. We could say they remained cucumbers.

What is the spiritual vinegar that completely changes you from a "cucumber" to a spiritual "pickle"? The baptism in the Holy Spirit. He enveloped the saints in the Upper Room and completely transformed them with His resurrection life, which makes dead things come alive. He brought the disciples out of their dark hiding place of fear and into the light and liberty of the Spirit. Suddenly they had no concern for themselves and their own personal safety. They were so full of resurrection life that they were consumed with getting everyone they met filled with resurrection life also.

There is only one baptism that makes you holy, and that is the baptism in the Holy Spirit. He gives you a brand-new spirit that is connected and alive to God. He comes to live inside you and immediately begins "redecorating" your inner being, which will affect your thoughts, your words, and your actions. Paul wrote in 1 Corinthians 12:13: "For by one Spirit we were all baptized into one body ... and have all been made to drink into one Spirit." We were spiritually pickled!

The Bible relates an incident when Paul instructs some disciples on this very thing:

Resurrection Life Endues You

And it happened, while Apollos was at Corinth, that Paul, having passed through the upper regions, came to Ephesus. And finding some disciples he said to them, "Did you receive the Holy Spirit when you believed?"

So they said to him, "We have not so much as heard whether there is a Holy Spirit."

And he said to them, "Into what then were you baptized?"

So they said, "Into John's baptism."

Then Paul said, "John indeed baptized with a baptism of repentance, saying to the people that they should believe on Him who would come after him, that is, on Christ Jesus."

Acts 19:1-4

Basically, Paul was asking these people, "Have you been pickled?" As it turned out, they only had been baptized in water. They were still spiritual cucumbers. They had repented of their sins and had been temporarily cleansed, but there had been no permanent change inside them. Paul tells them that there is much more for them to receive if they believe on the Lord Jesus Christ.

When they heard this, they were baptized in the name of the Lord Jesus. And when Paul had laid hands on them, the Holy Spirit came upon them, and they spoke with tongues and prophesied.

Acts 19:5-6

The Holy Spirit came upon them the same way He came upon the disciples in the Upper Room. He saturated them with resurrection life. They were permanently changed inside and outside, which was manifested and declared in tongues and prophecy. They had become spiritual pickles!

Resurrection Life Now!

It's Not a Suggestion

Behold, I send the Promise of My Father upon you; but tarry in the city of Jerusalem until you are endued with power from on high." And He led them out as far as Bethany, and He lifted up His hands and blessed them. Now it came to pass, while He blessed them, that He was parted from them and carried up into heaven.

Luke 24:49-51

It's amazing to me that believers can read this passage of Scripture and still maintain that they do not need the baptism of the Holy Spirit or to be "endued with power from on high." Frankly, you can usually tell those who have been baptized in the Holy Ghost and those who have not. Those who have are continuously looking for an opportunity to share the Gospel, talk about the Word of God, pray for the sick, give an encouraging word of prophecy, and even cast out a demon. Their greatest joy is talking about Jesus and doing the same works He did when He walked the Earth.

Those who have not been baptized in the Holy Spirit are like tamed lions, who have been trained by the world to keep quiet about their faith, believe that miracles are only a sovereign act of God's whim, and that being religious is a private matter. They are still hiding like the disciples did before the Upper Room. They need to have an Upper Room experience and receive the gift of the Holy Spirit! Then they will go out in the world in the full power of the resurrection life within them.

Jesus didn't suggest we receive the Promise of the Father; He commanded it. He commanded us to allow Him to immerse us in eternal life and resurrection life because this would endue us with power. The word translated "endued" is a lot like the word *baptizo*. It is the Greek word *enduo*: "... *to sink, go in or under, to put on. To enter, put on.... of a person as clothed, i.e., endued, furnished with any power.*"[4]

Jesus said we should be immersed in and also clothed with the resurrection power of the Holy Spirit. He commanded us to be clothed and immersed with power from on high, and the Greek word translated "power" in Luke 24:49 is dunamis, which means: "*Miraculous power ... ability, abundance, meaning, might ... power, strength, violence, mighty (wonderful) work.*"[5]

Beloved, you are not supposed to go anywhere or to do anything until you are immersed in and clothed with miracle-working power and supernatural strength, a power that comes from "on high," right from the heart and hand of God. Resurrection power comes from Heaven, from a dimension that is not of this world.

Can you see why I went from being a shy little girl to a bold preacher woman after I was baptized in the resurrection power of the Holy Spirit? Can you better understand the incredible difference the baptism of the Holy Spirit made in the lives of those first believers in the Upper Room?

Now imagine the difference He can make in your life!

Being a Witness

"But you shall receive power when the Holy Spirit has come upon you; and you shall be witnesses to Me in Jerusalem, and in all Judea and Samaria, and to the end of the earth."

Acts 1:8

There are always good reasons for anything Jesus commands us to do. The main reason we are to be endued with power from on high, to be clothed with and immersed in resurrection life, is so that we can be witnesses of our Lord Jesus Christ. However, being a witness may be a little different than what we have always thought.

When you are a witness in a court of law, you give your testimony concerning what you know to be "the truth, the whole truth, and nothing but the truth, so help you God." So being a witness for the living, resurrected Lord Jesus means telling people the truth about Him. He died on the cross to pay the price for their sins and rose from the dead to make them a new creation, a born-again human being, who is forgiven and restored to God the Father eternally, and who can walk in resurrection life now.

We are to testify to the truth of this Gospel to Jerusalem (our family and closest friends), Judea (our communities and cities), Samaria (foreign places that may or may not be hostile toward us), and "the end of the earth" (throughout the world, either by being missionaries or supporting missions). This is a lot to do, and I can tell you from years of experience that you cannot save anyone. Only God saves, but He does that through the power of the Holy Spirit working in and through you.

If you are not walking in the resurrection life of the Holy Spirit when you lean over your fence and tell your neighbor about Jesus, nothing may happen to your neighbor. Jesus said,

"It is the Spirit who gives life; the flesh profits nothing."

John 6:63

Your body can go to the mission field and your mouth can eloquently tell the Gospel story in the language of those unbelievers, but if you are not endued with power from on high, if you are just going through the motions in your flesh, you may be wasting your time and God's time.

Resurrection Life Endues You

On the other hand, if you lean across your fence or go to the mission field completely "pickled," clothed in the fire and glory of God, great things are definitely going to happen! The seed of the Word you plant in people's hearts is going to be filled with resurrection life, and you will have released the convicting power of the Holy Spirit to do what He does best: save the lost. You will find you are supernaturally empowered to share the Lord Jesus Christ with others.

I found this out not long after I received the gift of the Holy Spirit. I had committed myself to go into full-time ministry whenever the Lord opened the door. He had said to me, "If you'll do what I'm calling you to do, I will save everyone in your family. But if you don't, you'll be in the way, and I'll have to deal with you." Needless to say, I was afraid not to obey God!

Shortly after He spoke that to me, an opportunity came for me to be a youth pastor at a church in Houston, so I quit my job to answer that call. Just before that, I was asked to preach a meeting at the church I had gotten saved in as a child, in Channelview, Texas, where Bethel Hagee, the father of John Hagee, was pastoring. These two commitments are exactly what I'm talking about when I say that the resurrection power of the Holy Spirit will give you the courage and strength to pull up all your roots and move to another job or city or even country. He also will empower you in ways you cannot imagine when you step out in faith and do something you have never done before.

I didn't know what a revival was, but I soon found out. The meetings in Channelview started out with about thirty people in an old theater that had been made into a church. The meetings kept going on, day and night, and by Friday night the place was packed full. By the end of the week I had preached thirteen times! They had me speaking every morning and evening. I said, "God, I wanted to preach, but I didn't want to die in the first revival!"

Resurrection Life Now!

There is no way you can obey God in these ways and see such incredible results without the gift of the Holy Spirit. I know that I could not have quit my job and moved to another city, nor could I have had the strength—both physical and spiritual—to do thirteen meetings in a week, without being "endued with power from on high." During that revival, I surely got tired, but I would pray in the Spirit and draw upon God's Word, and the joy of the Lord was my strength.

How Do You Know You Got It?

Of course, the main thing that tells you the Holy Spirit has endued you with power from on high is the new fire in your belly. Like the disciples on the Day of Pentecost, you want to tell everyone you meet about the saving grace of the Lord Jesus Christ. But if Jesus baptizes you in the Holy Spirit at 3 a.m. and there is no one to run out and tell, something else will happen that will seal the deal. Like the disciples in the Upper Room, you will speak with new tongues and the glory of God will engulf you. You will have a new spiritual language with which to communicate with Him.

Years ago, my husband John and I prayed and asked God how He wanted us to lead people in the baptism of the Holy Spirit. He told us that when someone in our church or our various outreach ministries came to the Lord, we were to instruct them to come to the church to be water baptized immediately. We obeyed His instructions in faith.

The next time some people got saved, we explained that Jesus commanded every new believer to be water baptized. We showed them this in the Bible and then showed them what happened to the saints on the Day of Pentecost. From the first person we baptized in water, we witnessed an astounding phenomenon. These new converts would go under the water holding their noses and come out of the water speaking in tongues! And we have seen this happen ever since.

Resurrection Life Endues You

Now my sister's husband, Dick, had a different experience. Before I was married, Dick was determined to prove that my sister and I were wrong about being filled with the Holy Spirit. He was going to a little denominational church, but my sister was going with me to a little Pentecostal church. He was sure we didn't know what we were doing, and he was excited because his church was going to have a class on why speaking in tongues was not for today. He was going to get fully loaded with Scripture and let us have it!

As usual, God had something else in mind when Dick attended that class. He came home one evening and said to my sister, "We've got to find another church."

She asked, "Why? What happened?"

"Well, we were reading the second chapter of Acts, where it says the Holy Spirit came on them, and they skipped the rest of the verse that said they spoke in tongues. They just skipped that part of the Bible. They wouldn't read or talk about all that the Scriptures said."

About midnight my telephone rang. It was my sister. She said, "Guess what?" And I thought, *Oh, no. Oh, no.* When you get a phone call at midnight, you immediately think something bad has happened. She went right on, "Dick was filled with the Holy Spirit tonight."

I said, "Put him on the phone." She put him on the phone, and I said, "What happened to you?"

He said, "I don't know, but it started in my feet and it came out my mouth." And this was one who said tongues couldn't possibly be for today! God had brought him right around to take a good look at His Word. When Dick saw what the Word actually said and came out from under the influence of those who were walking in unbelief toward the truth, he easily received everything God wanted to give him right in his own home.

Resurrection Life Now!

I'm telling you this because it doesn't matter where you are or what you're doing. And you don't need a preacher to lay hands on you or to be baptized in water again to be baptized in the Holy Spirit and be endued with power from on high. Jesus can immerse, clothe, and "pickle" you, releasing your heavenly language of tongues, anywhere, anytime. Just ask Him! And if you are having any trouble receiving, go to a pastor or another mature Christian who believes this truth and walks in it.

Most of all, always remember that Jesus wants you to have the gift of the Holy Spirit! Think about this: When a baby begins to speak, who is that baby talking to? Mama and Daddy. When you are born again, a babe in Christ, who do you talk to? You begin to speak in a heavenly language to your Abba, Father!

Another thing I understand is that before babies are born, they can hear. As soon as the Holy Spirit fills you, you begin to hear in your spirit. You say, "You know, I just feel like God's saying this to me, like He wants me to know this." You are developing your sense of spiritual hearing. You are born again with a capacity to know your Father and to communicate with Him—just like Adam and Eve did in the garden before the Fall.

Jesus wants you to have the gift of the Holy Spirit because He is your powerful communication connection with the Father. Praying in the Spirit is a major key to walking in the resurrection life He died to give you and becoming a powerful witness for Him. You can resist temptation and sin. You can refuse to fall for the seductions and deceptions of this world and the lies and wiles of the devil. You can know His will for your life and do it. All these things are part of your testimony to the truth of the Gospel of the Lord Jesus Christ.

As I wrote in the beginning of this chapter, you are more than you think you are. All you need is to be endued with power from on high!

Chapter 5

Resurrection Life Empowers You

There is another part of being a witness for the Lord Jesus Christ that happens when you are endued with power on high. Not only do you have a passion to see the lost come to Jesus, to preach the truth of God's Word and for your life to be a powerful witness to the truth, but also you have new tools with which to do that. Before Jesus ascended He commissioned the Church:

> "And these signs will follow those who believe: In My name they will cast out demons; they will speak with new tongues; they will take up serpents; and if they drink anything deadly, it will by no means hurt them; they will lay hands on the sick, and they will recover."
>
> *Mark 16:17-18*

WOW! That's quite a toolbox!

Notice that He said these signs would follow us—we don't run after them. They just happen when we obey the leading of the Spirit and the Word of God. But they only follow "those who believe." What are we supposed to believe? We are supposed to believe that Jesus was raised from the dead and is alive forevermore. In fact, in verse 14, just before He spoke the words above, Jesus "...*rebuked their unbelief and hardness of heart, because they did not believe those who had seen Him after He had risen."*

Obviously, there is a dynamic connection between believing Jesus was resurrected and all these miraculous signs following us.

The Purpose of Signs

Let's stop a minute to consider what signs do. On the highway, they tell you where you are. They let you know where you are going. They warn you about potentially dangerous situations. They even tell you how fast you should be going. There are also big billboard signs that encourage you to buy or do something. Overall, signs give you valuable and life-saving information. So we have to ask ourselves what valuable and life-saving information the signs in Mark 16:17-18 give.

Jesus was telling the disciples that casting out demons, speaking with new tongues, not being hurt by snakes or poison of any kind, and healing the sick were signs pointing to His resurrection—they demonstrate the resurrection life He died to give us! They give this valuable and life-saving information to the unbeliever: "He is risen, and you can be forgiven and saved from eternal damnation. You can be restored to the Father and be delivered from the sin, sickness, and demonic powers of darkness that are killing you. You too can have resurrection life!"

Every time we speak in tongues or heal the sick, it is not to show how spiritual and holy we are; it is to demonstrate the resurrection life of our Lord Jesus Christ!

An example of this was a gift the Holy Spirit operated through my husband. When we were in Israel with a group from our church, we were praying in what they believe to be the Upper Room. Suddenly my husband began to speak in tongues, very quietly at first and then in a distinctly louder voice. Afterwards our guide, who was Arab, asked my husband where he had learned that Indian dialect. John said that he did not know it. Very emphatically, the guide said, "You prayed in an Indian dialect." There are hundreds of Indian dialects, but John prayed in the one the guide understood.

This didn't happen so that John could prove how spiritual he was. The Holy Spirit operated one of the gifts of the Spirit through John to reach out to our Arab guide. John's "tongue" was a sign to him that John's Lord Jesus was the resurrection and the life.

The Restoration of Spiritual Gifts

When Adam fell, mankind lost their spiritual abilities; through Jesus Christ, our spiritual abilities are restored. The resurrection life He died to give us includes the gifts of the Spirit as well as the fruit of the Spirit. We must persevere in becoming mature in the power of the Holy Spirit as well as the character of Christ.

I always wanted to know what Adam knew before he fell, and I got the answer when I read 1 Corinthians 12. I realized he functioned in the nine gifts of the Spirit as well as the nine fruit of the Spirit. He lived his life by his spirit, and that's the way we are supposed to live. Since God knows everything, by communicating with Him in the Spirit we can know things, see things, hear things, and sense things we could not possibly experience through our physical senses.

In case you are wondering if all these supernatural abilities are necessary to the Christian life, here is what the apostle Paul had to say about it:

Now concerning spiritual gifts, brethren, I do not want you to be ignorant.

1 Corinthians 12:1

Ignorance can mean everything from never having heard of it to knowing just enough about it to get you killed, but in the Bible it is always referring to spiritual darkness. Ignorance is not a godly trait because God is omniscient—all-knowing—and you are His child. He wants you to be knowledgeable and to have understanding about Him and everything that concerns you in the life He has given you. He tells you in Hosea 4:6 that you will be destroyed if you are ignorant, and that includes being ignorant of the spiritual gifts. We all need to learn everything we can about them.

Paul goes on to describe these gifts.

But the manifestation of the Spirit is given to each one for the profit of all: for to one is given the word of wisdom through the Spirit, to another the word of knowledge through the same Spirit, to another faith by the same Spirit, to another gifts of healings by the same Spirit, to another the working of miracles, to another prophecy, to another discerning of spirits, to another different kinds of tongues, to another the interpretation of tongues.

1 Corinthians 12:7-9

As a child of God, you are a spiritual being, and you possess spiritual abilities that the Bible refers to as a "manifestation of the Spirit." In other words, the gifts named above appear in your life by the working of the Holy Spirit, the resurrection life within you. Furthermore, every believer has the capability of moving in these gifts. "But the manifestation of the Spirit is given to each one" (verse 7 above).

Why did God give these gifts to us? Verse 7 goes on to say "for the profit of all." These gifts will profit you and everyone around you. As we discussed before, they are signs that point to the resurrection of Jesus Christ because they are a manifestation of the resurrection life within you.

Resurrection Life Empowers You

What are these gifts? There are nine of them, just like there are nine fruit of the Spirit:

- word of wisdom – reveals God's will and way
- word of knowledge – provides vital information
- faith – supernatural ability to believe God can do the impossible and overcome any natural obstacle
- gifts of healings – miraculous restoration of the body in various ways
- working of miracles – a manifestation of power that overcomes natural law
- prophecy – edification (instruction), exhortation (inspiration and advice), and comfort regarding the future
- discerning of spirits – identifying evil spirits or the spiritual condition of another person
- different kinds of tongues – heavenly language or earthly language that you do not understand
- interpretation of tongues – meaning of a message in tongues, which has been given in a language no one understands

You may think, I'll leave all that up to the pastor, the elders, and the evangelists. You don't need to because you're a spirit being! You are like Jesus: You live in a robe of clay, but you are primarily a spirit, and you are not to be ignorant about these gifts; you are to be educated about them and operate in them.

Now the word translated "spiritual gifts" in 1 Corinthians 12:1 is *pneumatikos*, which simply means spiritual or supernatural.[1] You will notice in many versions that the word "gifts" is italicized. That is because it is not in the original Greek text. If we were to translate this correctly, we would say, "Now concerning that which is spiritual or supernatural about your lives, brethren, I do not want you to be ignorant." However, the translators were not wrong, because verse 4 reads, *There are diversities of gifts, but the same Spirit.*

The word "gifts" (which is in the text) is *charisma*, which means "grace or gifts denoting extraordinary powers."[2] We go on to verses 7-9 and find out that there are nine of these spiritual gifts and extraordinary powers or abilities.

If you're like me, you've always wanted to be very spiritual and operate in great supernatural abilities. You want the gifts of healing and miracles. You want to prophesy and desire for the Holy Spirit to use you in a mighty way. However, one of the things Paul tells us right away is that we can't produce a word of knowledge, prophesy, or manufacture the gift of faith. We can't manifest any of the gifts of the Spirit in our own abilities because the gifts are spiritual, supernatural. They are also gifts. That means they are given as the Spirit wills. The Holy Spirit decides when, where, who, and what gift.

> *But one and the same Spirit works all these things, distributing to each one individually as He wills.*
>
> *1 Corinthians 12:11*

Your part is to walk in resurrection life, because this is how the Holy Spirit can manifest His power through you. This is how you do the works of Jesus. Maybe you thought, I don't know how to do a miracle. How will I ever heal the sick or prophesy? And what is the gift of faith, anyway? I have great news for you: It's not up to you. The only thing you have to do is make yourself available to the Holy Spirit, and He will do the rest.

At the right time and the right place, to the right person or persons, the Holy Spirit will manifest His resurrection power through you in one of His gifts. It never can be your power and ability. It will always be the Holy Spirit's. You just make sure you are willing and obedient, and then He will manifest the gifts through you as He wills. If you will He will!

Resurrection Life Empowers You

The first Adam had these abilities and lost them. You want to know what Adam used to know? Read the list of nine gifts of the Spirit above. He had the wisdom and knowledge to name all the animals. He didn't have a biology textbook to read or a degree from a university. He was spiritually one with the Creator of the universe and had His Spirit living inside him. The Holy Spirit was the source of Adam's spiritual abilities, and we've been restored to where the first Adam was through the last Adam. Jesus Christ has brought us back into that spiritual relationship with the Father and filled us with His resurrection life—a life of signs and wonders following!

So let us take a closer look at how God wants to manifest the resurrection life of His Son through us.

Word of Wisdom – Reveals God's Will and Way

This is not human wisdom. This is a wisdom that comes when we are filled with the Holy Spirit. We will understand something by the Spirit that we couldn't possibly have understood through our five senses. We know it in our spirit because the Holy Spirit is empowering us to understand something we could never understand in our natural reasoning.

When God gives you a word of wisdom, it is wisdom to do His will, wisdom that you do not have on your own. When my daughter was eighteen, she was sick and the doctors could not figure out what was wrong. After many tests and treatments, they decided she had Lyme disease. She had broken out in what looked like chicken pox, but the marks became craters. Each crater had a large red ring the size of a fifty-cent piece around it.

It "came to me" in my spirit to tell her to get in the bathtub and put regular soda in the tepid water, and to do this several times a day. She did this, and after a week the skin problem was gone. I believe the Holy

Spirit gave me wisdom I did not have on my own about what to do to help her. He gave me a word of wisdom as a gift to my daughter. Do you see why He calls them gifts?

Word of Knowledge – Provides Vital Information

God will give you knowledge about a situation that you have no way of knowing on your own. In the Bible, for example, when they gave an offering to the church, Ananais and Sapphira lied about the price of land they sold. The Spirit of God revealed to Peter that they were lying:

> But a certain man named Ananias, with Sapphira his wife, sold a possession. And he kept back part of the proceeds, his wife also being aware of it, and brought a certain part and laid it at the apostles' feet. But Peter said, "Ananias, why has Satan filled your heart to lie to the Holy Spirit and keep back part of the price of the land for yourself?"
>
> *Acts 5:1-3*

Peter knew by the Spirit what he could not have known through any natural means. That is the gift of a word of knowledge.

Faith – Supernatural Ability to Believe God Can Do the Impossible and Overcome Any Natural Obstacle

Faith comes by hearing a word from God. When you know in your heart you have heard God on a situation, you can step out of the boat like Peter did and walk on water.

> And Peter answered Him and said, "Lord, if it is You, command me to come to You on the water." So He said, "Come." And when Peter had come down out of the boat, he walked on the water to go to Jesus.
>
> *Matthew 14:28-29*

Resurrection Life Empowers You

When the Holy Spirit gives you the gift of faith, there will be a reason for it! He will also tell you what He wants you to pray and believe or do, and it will be something you could not possibly do without His supernatural ability. That's why you need faith that goes far beyond the "everyday." The gift of faith is awesome!

Gifts of Healings – Miraculous Restoration of the Physical Body in Various Ways

Through my life as a believer and in ministry, I have witnessed all kinds of healings that were accomplished in all kinds of ways. I was there when a large cancer on a man's face fell off as the minister prayed for him. I have seen huge growths disappear and new organs appear. Although the amazing healings I have witnessed have come about in different ways by different ministers, they were all empowered by the same Holy Spirit.

There are diversities of gifts, but the same Spirit.

But one and the same Spirit works all these things, distributing to each one individually as He wills.

1 Corinthians 12:4, 11

Recovery from a sickness, disease, or accident can come through doctors and natural medicine, but whenever the gift of healing operates in a believer, it is supernatural. It is by the empowerment of the Holy Spirit.

Working of Miracles – A Manifestation of God's Power that Overcomes Natural Law

In a tent meeting in Atlanta, Georgia, I saw a man who had fallen through a plate glass door and had almost cut his arm off go up for prayer. His arm had been sewed back on and was in a cast, but it was not healing and was getting worse. Doctors had told him the arm would have to be amputated within two days or he would die of blood poisoning. As the minister began to pray for this man, his hand, which had been black as coal, became flesh colored immediately. He came back the next night with the cast off and praising God for His miracle.

I believe God loves to do miracles for people. He loves to calm storms, raise people from the dead, and even stop the sun from going down for a day, like he did for Joshua in Joshua 10:12-13. He loves to do miracles through His people.

Prophecy – Edification (instruction), Exhortation (inspiration and advice), and Comfort Regarding the Future

A prophetic word was given to me when I was seventeen, and it changed the course of my life. God spoke to me through the prophets that I was called to preach. I had already felt this as a little girl, but when it was confirmed in these words of prophecy, I never doubted my call and lived my life in full confidence that I was in God's will.

This gift is one that Paul urges all of us to seek: "Pursue love, and desire spiritual gifts, but especially that you may prophesy" (1 Corinthians 14:1). There is nothing more affirming than confirmation that you are on the right path, that your dream is God's dream for you, or that the suffering you are enduring will end and everything will be okay.

This gift is also a tremendous tool for us with unbelievers, who cannot hear and commune with God the way we do. We can give them a word from the Lord, something only God would know about them and something we could never have known, and they will be stunned by the fact that He not only sees everything in their heart and life, but also He loves them and cares for them enough to have us speak to them on His behalf.

In the Church, we still need edification, exhortation, and comfort. We are born again and filled with the Spirit, but we are also still walking in this robe of clay. God placed us in a body of believers because we cannot live this resurrection life without each other, and this is one of the gifts that prove it!

Discerning of Spirits – Identifying Evil Spirits or the Spiritual Condition of Another Person

This is the supernatural ability to detect the presence of demons and identify evil forces at work in people's lives. The apostle Paul experienced this when a young girl kept following him all over Philippi. At first she seemed to be encouraging him, but it wasn't long before he became irritated by her pronouncements, and the Holy Spirit showed him that she was demon possessed.

> *Now it happened, as we went to prayer, that a certain slave girl possessed with a spirit of divination met us, who brought her masters much profit by fortune-telling. This girl followed Paul and us, and cried out, saying, "These men are the servants of the Most High God, who proclaim to us the way of salvation." And this she did for many days.*
>
> *But Paul, greatly annoyed, turned and said to the spirit, "I command you in the name of Jesus Christ to come out of her." And he came out that very hour.*
>
> *Acts 16:16-18*

The Holy Spirit delivered this girl by operating the gift of discerning of spirits through Paul. Paul did not "get it" until the Holy Spirit caused such an annoyance in Paul's spirit that he realized the girl was in spiritual bondage. Notice that Paul didn't turn to his believing friends and tell them about the terrible condition of this poor girl, nor did he call a meeting to analyze the situation and make a plan. No! He just turned around and told the evil spirit to come out.

This gift is not to gossip about anyone or judge and be critical of those who are oppressed or possessed by demonic powers. It's not to show other believers how spiritual you are. This gift, like all the gifts, is to reveal the resurrection life of Christ Jesus that sets people free!

Different Kinds of Tongues – Heavenly Language or Earthly Language that You Do Not Understand

One Tuesday morning after our Bible study at the church, an elderly woman was brought in the side door. We did not know her, but those who brought her said she needed prayer. My husband and others gathered around her and began to pray. John simply prayed in the Spirit over her. The next day the woman called the church office and wanted to know where Pastor John had learned Hebrew. She said when he prayed for her, he had prayed in perfect Hebrew. John did not know and had never studied Hebrew.

The Holy Spirit had given John the gift of tongues in an earthly language that only this woman could understand. This was a gift my husband would move in from time to time, and it is always a powerful witness to the hearer that the resurrection life of Jesus Christ is not only powerful, but that God loves and cares for them enough to do something supernatural to reach out to them.

Interpretation of Tongues – Meaning of a Message in Tongues, Which Has Been Given in a Language No One Understands

The interpretation of a tongue is usually not given when the tongue spoken is an earthly language, such as was the case when my husband spoke a message in a tongue he did not understand, but someone else did understand it. An interpretation is usually given when the message in tongues is a heavenly language, one no one would understand but the Holy Spirit. The Holy Spirit might give the interpretation to the person who gave the message in tongues, or He might give it to someone else, but the Bible instructs us to always interpret this kind of tongue:

> *Therefore let him who speaks in a tongue pray that he may interpret.*
>
> *1 Corinthians 14:13*

Paul was so strong on this! In 1 Corinthians 14, he reminds us that there are several kinds of tongues. Your prayer language edifies you by connecting you to God in an intimate way. Sometimes the Holy Spirit will give you the interpretation of what you are praying, and sometimes it is just a powerful means to build your faith in your inner being (Jude 1:20).

In Romans 8:26, the Bible also says that when you don't know how to pray or what to pray, the Holy Spirit can pray the perfect will of God through you, sometimes with groanings. With this kind of tongue, you usually pray until your spirit and soul are flooded with peace, which lets you know you are finished praying. The Holy Spirit has accomplished what He intended to accomplish through you.

Sometimes I will wake up in the middle of the night, praying in the Spirit, and have no idea what or who I'm praying for. When that peace that passes all understanding comes over me, I know God has had His way, and I can go back to sleep.

When you pray in tongues in a group of believers, and it is obviously a message that stands out because the Holy Spirit is speaking something to the entire group, that message must be interpreted; otherwise, no one will understand what the Holy Spirit is saying. Paul wrote:

> But now, brethren, if I come to you speaking with tongues, what shall I profit you unless I speak to you either by revelation, by knowledge, by prophesying, or by teaching? So likewise you, unless you utter by the tongue words easy to understand, how will it be known what is spoken? For you will be speaking into the air.
>
> *1 Corinthians 14:6-9,13*

When more than one believer begins to speak in their heavenly prayer language of tongues, they can do so to build up their faith. But when the Holy Spirit begins to give one of them a message to the group in a tongue, it must be interpreted; or else, as Paul says, the tongue is not understood by anyone and the Holy Spirit has not been able to speak to anyone. That person is "speaking into the air," and what they are saying is just nonsense.

There are many wonderful books about the gifts of the Spirit and how the Church is to operate in them, probably because there is just as much controversy and trouble regarding the gifts of the Spirit in our day as there was in Paul's day! One thing is certain: The gifts were real then, and they are real today! As God's children, we need to desire these gifts, and that means giving full rein to the resurrection life of the Holy Spirit inside us.

Decently and in Order

One of the places the Church always seems to get into trouble, from after the Day of Pentecost until now, is with the gifts of the Spirit. Today, I find that churches either don't teach them, they don't allow the Holy Spirit to operate the gifts in their congregations, or they are like the Corinthians and go to extremes, causing confusion and chaos in the services. What we need to do, Beloved, is stick to what the Bible tells us about these gifts and always be willing to let the Holy Spirit use us. Why? Because, as you can tell from some of the experiences I related earlier, they can save someone's life!

The apostle Paul exhorts us that the Lord wants to speak to us in this way:

> Brethren, do not be children in understanding; however, in malice be babes, but in understanding be mature.
>
> In the law it is written:
>
> "With men of other tongues and other lips I will speak to this people; And yet, for all that, they will not hear Me," says the Lord.
>
> Therefore tongues are for a sign, not to those who believe but to unbelievers; but prophesying is not for unbelievers but for those who believe. Therefore if the whole church comes together in one place, and all speak with tongues, and there come in those who are uninformed or unbelievers, will they not say that you are out of your mind? But if all prophesy, and an unbeliever or an uninformed person comes in, he is convinced by all, he is convicted by all. And thus the secrets of his heart are revealed; and so, falling down on his face, he will worship God and report that God is truly among you.
>
> *1 Corinthians 14:20-25*

When was the last time you saw an unbeliever fall on his face, worship God, and declare that God was in the midst of your congregation of saints? Wouldn't you like to see that on a regular basis? I know I would! The Lord wants to convict unbelievers and bring them into His kingdom through the operation of the gifts of the Spirit, but we have to be willing to let the Holy Spirit move in our midst.

Resurrection Life Now!

We also need to do things God's way. We have to understand that He has an orderly way of operating in these gifts.

How is it then, brethren? Whenever you come together, each of you has a psalm, has a teaching, has a tongue, has a revelation, has an interpretation. Let all things be done for edification. If anyone speaks in a tongue, let there be two or at the most three, each in turn, and let one interpret. But if there is no interpreter, let him keep silent in church, and let him speak to himself and to God. Let two or three prophets speak, and let the others judge. But if anything is revealed to another who sits by, let the first keep silent. For you can all prophesy one by one, that all may learn and all may be encouraged.

1 Corinthians 14:26-31

Up to three people can give a message in tongues, and then the interpretation must be given. And they can't all talk at the same time! Moreover, if you give a message in tongues to the whole church or a group of believers, you must be ready to interpret; otherwise, keep your mouth shut. This passage also says that two or three prophets could speak, one at a time, and other prophets and believers can judge the prophetic words given.

There must have been a lot of disorderly behavior in the Corinthian church for Paul to get this detailed, but we need to follow these instructions in our churches too.

Therefore, brethren, desire earnestly to prophesy, and do not forbid to speak with tongues. Let all things be done decently and in order.

1 Corinthians 14:39-40

Resurrection Life Empowers You

We've covered the issue of doing things in God's order, but what does it mean by doing things decently? It means we have to have the right heart motivation. These gifts are operated by the Holy Spirit not us. We don't submit to Him and develop the gifts He's given us to glorify and exalt ourselves, but we are to submit to Him in these gifts in order to bless others and declare the resurrection life of Jesus Christ.

The bottom line is that we are to encourage and help one another when we are fellowshipping among ourselves, and we are to bless unbelievers (although they may not see it that way at first) by the gifts of the Spirit so they can see there is a God, He loves them, He knows them better than they know themselves, and He wants to save them and be a part of their lives.

We aren't supposed to get up and act superspiritual, tell one another's business in public, and try to control people by our gifts. We are to be humble and helpful, knowing it isn't us who are speaking or healing or doing the miracle; it is the Holy Spirit on the inside of us. He is pouring His resurrection life out of us into the lives of those around us so that they can be saved, healed, delivered, and set free.

Jesus Is Our Resurrection Life Now

God wants to move through us. He wants to reveal Himself to the lost in our lives through the gifts of the Spirit. He wants to empower us to supernaturally bless our brothers and sisters in the Lord who are sick, confused, or ready to throw in the towel and quit. The gifts of the Spirit are for both the lost and the saved. Jesus healed those who didn't believe in Him and those who did. He did miracles in front of the people who hated Him as well as the people who loved Him. Everywhere He went, He not only spoke but demonstrated that He was the resurrection and the life they needed.

Resurrection Life Now!

When Jesus got the message that His good friend Lazarus had died, He did something no one understood: He didn't come to Lazarus' home right away. By the time He got there, Lazarus had been dead for four days! This was important because the Jews believed that the spirit of the dead hung around for three days, but after that, the spirit left for good and there was no chance of the person being revived.

Lazarus' two sisters, Mary and Martha, were beside themselves by the time Jesus arrived. In fact, they were angry with Him. Each of them said, "Lord, if You had been here, my brother would not have died" (John 11:21, 32). Martha is the one who caught hold of the resurrection life in Jesus, however. She said,

> *"Lord, if You had been here, my brother would not have died. But even now I know that whatever You ask of God, God will give You."*
>
> *Jesus said to her, "Your brother will rise again."*
>
> *Martha said to Him, "I know that he will rise again in the resurrection at the last day."*
>
> *Jesus said to her, "I am the resurrection and the life. He who believes in Me, though he may die, he shall live. And whoever lives and believes in Me shall never die. Do you believe this?"*
>
> *She said to Him, "Yes, Lord, I believe that You are the Christ, the Son of God, who is to come into the world."*
>
> *John 11:21-27*

Martha believed Jesus was not just a great prophet and miracle-worker; she believed He was the Son of God, the Anointed One, the Messiah who was the life-giving Spirit. She believed Him when He said He was the resurrection and the life.

Resurrection Life Empowers You

Look at what happens when we believe that Jesus is the resurrection and the life—making dead things alive:

And Jesus lifted up His eyes and said, "Father, I thank You that You have heard Me. And I know that You always hear Me, but because of the people who are standing by I said this, that they may believe that You sent Me." Now when He had said these things, He cried with a loud voice, "Lazarus, come forth!" And he who had died came out bound hand and foot with grave-clothes, and his face was wrapped with a cloth. Jesus said to them, "Loose him, and let him go."

John 11:41-44

Hallelujah! The dead was made alive, loosed, and set free by the resurrection power of the Holy Spirit. Jesus was empowered by the Spirit in the gift of miracles.

You may say, "But Pastor Anne, Jesus was the Son of God. He didn't operate in the gifts of the Spirit." Think again! Jesus said in John 8:28, "I do nothing of Myself." And in Philippians 2:5-8, it says:

Have this attitude in yourselves which was also in Christ Jesus, who, although He existed in the form of God, did not regard equality with God a thing to be grasped, but emptied Himself, taking the form of a bond-servant, and being made in the likeness of men. Being found in appearance as a man, He humbled Himself by becoming obedient to the point of death, even death on a cross.

Jesus was 100 percent God and 100 percent human, but while He walked this earth in His robe of clay, He lived as a human being who was empowered by the Holy Spirit. Looking forward to His resurrection before Him, knowing He was slain from before the foundation of the world, He lived in resurrection life now. He walked as a humble servant of His Father, doing the Father's will in the power of the Holy Spirit, who was in Him and upon Him. And we are to be like Him today.

How do you do the works of Jesus? How do you operate in and develop these spiritual gifts in your life? The gifts of the Spirit have nothing to do with flesh and blood. They have everything to do with the One who lives on the inside of you. You see, your reconnection with God through the Holy Spirit means you are like Jesus, and He was always about His Father's business, empowered by the Spirit of God in Him and upon Him. You are to follow Jesus in every aspect of your life, so you are empowered by the Holy Spirit too.

You Are a Gift

Jesus walked in all the gifts of the Holy Spirit, but you may only walk in some of them—that's up to the Holy Spirit. But you can pray without ceasing, keep your mind renewed and meditating on God's Word, and just be quiet inside, listening for His voice and waiting on His unction to move in one of the nine spiritual gifts. Along with these nine gifts, the Bible lists some others that we call ministry gifts. They are also empowered by the Holy Spirit.

Here are the passages of Scripture that list these other gifts:

Now you are the body of Christ, and members individually. And God has appointed these in the church: first apostles, second prophets, third teachers, after that miracles, then gifts of healings, helps, administrations, varieties of tongues. Are all apostles? Are all prophets? Are all teachers? Are all workers of miracles? Do all have gifts of healings? Do all speak with tongues? Do all interpret? But earnestly desire the best gifts.

1 Corinthians 12:27-31

Resurrection Life Empowers You

"When He ascended on high, He led captivity captive, and gave gifts to men."

And He Himself gave some to be apostles, some prophets, some evangelists, and some pastors and teachers, for the equipping of the saints for the work of ministry, for the edifying of the body of Christ, till we all come to the unity of the faith and of the knowledge of the Son of God, to a perfect man, to the measure of the stature of the fullness of Christ; that we should no longer be children, tossed to and fro and carried about with every wind of doctrine, by the trickery of men, in the cunning craftiness of deceitful plotting, but, speaking the truth in love, may grow up in all things into Him who is the head—Christ— from whom the whole body, joined and knit together by what every joint supplies, according to the effective working by which every part does its share, causes growth of the body for the edifying of itself in love.

Ephesians 4:8, 11-16

For as we have many members in one body, but all the members do not have the same function, so we, being many, are one body in Christ, and individually members of one another. Having then gifts differing according to the grace that is given to us, let us use them: if prophecy, let us prophesy in proportion to our faith; or ministry, let us use it in our ministering; he who teaches, in teaching; he who exhorts, in exhortation; he who gives, with liberality; he who leads, with diligence; he who shows mercy, with cheerfulness.

Romans 12:4-8

Resurrection Life Now!

Not only may the Holy Spirit use you to bless other people through the nine gifts of the Spirit, but you yourself are a spiritual gift! We are all ministers who have ministry gifts. Like me, you might be a pastor, a preacher, or a teacher. You might be a healing evangelist or an administrator, overseeing a department in your church or place of business. Or, you might be a successful business person, who funds church projects and the work of various ministries.

All these ministry gifts are spiritual callings, and they are given by God. You cannot just decide you are going to be an apostle or have a certain gift of the Spirit one day. God gives these gifts to the Church. It is His decision.

You can see that along with the nine gifts of the Spirit, members of the body of Christ help each other to carry out their ministries and live their lives. You have teachers to break the bread of life, the Word of God, into pieces you can chew and digest. You have apostles, who establish sound doctrine, provide accountability to leaders, and build strong churches. I'm not talking about just physical buildings but strong and effective bodies of believers. There are prophets to point the way when you are wondering if you are really hearing from God, and your pastors are there to comfort you, encourage you, and let you know when you need to address something in your life. You even have evangelists to help you to win the lost in your city.

You are probably asking, "How do I know my gifts?" Or you may be asking, "How do I fulfill my calling and 'stir up my gifts?'" The answer to each question is the same: The Word and prayer! The Word will build your faith and the mind of Christ inside you, and prayer in both your spoken language and your heavenly language connects you to the resurrection life of the Spirit, who empowers you in everything you do for God.

Resurrection Life Empowers You

You can pour out your heart to God in your language or your heavenly language. You can pray and declare God's Word in faith. And when you speak in tongues as the Spirit gives you utterance, it will open your heart and mind in such a way that the Holy Spirit can use you as He wills. You are operating in the same resurrection life Jesus operated in, and you are walking in the spiritual dimension all God's children were born again to walk in.

When you pray in the Spirit, you stir up the gift that's in you. You may not feel spiritual when you start to pray, but as you persevere in seeking the Lord, the Holy Spirit will be activated and released to empower and develop the gifts He has given you. It won't be long before you get fervent, with a fire in your belly! You will know you are standing in the throne room of grace, and all the power of Heaven is ready to bless you in whatever God has called you to do.

I think the Church has come through a season of, "What's my gift? What's my calling?" To a certain extent we've been like little chickens running around, trying this and trying that. But what we have come to realize is that winning the world is not going to be accomplished by any one person. We will do this together, our gifts and callings working together as Jesus' physical and spiritual body on the earth.

Remember what you read in Ephesians 4:8-16? The purpose of our gifts and callings is to help the body of Christ grow up in love, wisdom, stability, and become spiritually mature. "Till we all come to the unity of the faith and of the knowledge of the Son of God, to a perfect man, to the measure of the stature of the fullness of Christ ... according to the effective working by which every part does its share."

When we all do our part, empowered by the resurrection life within us right now, the world will see the mature Bride of Christ on the earth—and what a sight that will be!

Resurrection Life Now!

Chapter 6

Resurrection Life Enlightens You

But when Paul had gathered a bundle of sticks and laid them on the fire, a viper came out because of the heat, and fastened on his hand. So when the natives saw the creature hanging from his hand, they said to one another, "No doubt this man is a murderer, whom, though he has escaped the sea, yet justice does not allow to live." But he shook off the creature into the fire and suffered no harm. However, they were expecting that he would swell up or suddenly fall down dead. But after they had looked for a long time and saw no harm come to him, they changed their minds and said that he was a god.

Acts 28:3-6

Paul had just gone through the traumatic experience of a terrible storm at sea, being shipwrecked, and swimming to shore. He was exhausted, cold, and probably all he could think about was making a fire to get warm. As the fire was kindled, the heat caused a viper to come out of the pile of wood, and the snake sunk his poisonous fangs into Paul's hand.

Now if that had been me, after going through everything Paul had just gone through, I probably would have cried and said, "Okay Lord, just take me home." But what did Paul do? He flung off the snake. And then, when everyone expected him to swell up and die, he never did—he just kept going! How could he have reacted like this?

I'll tell you how. He knew there was resurrection life in him! He lived from the fullness of the Spirit of God inside him. He had such a revelation of his all-powerful and almighty God, and he walked in total faith and trust in Him. Do you see why Paul prayed for us,

> *Therefore I also, after I heard of your faith in the Lord Jesus and your love for all the saints, do not cease to give thanks for you, making mention of you in my prayers: that the God of our Lord Jesus Christ, the Father of glory, may give to you the spirit of wisdom and revelation in the knowledge of Him, the eyes of your understanding being enlightened.*
>
> *Ephesians 1:15-18*

Paul said, "I'm praying God will open your eyes." He spoke of the eyes of your understanding as your spiritual perception, the part of you that would grow in God's wisdom and revelation as you know Him better and better. Later in this passage, he said that one of the main things he wanted us to know about God is this:

> *...the exceeding greatness of His power toward us who believe, according to the working of His mighty power which He worked in Christ when He raised Him from the dead.*
>
> *Ephesians 1:19-20*

The "exceeding greatness of His power toward us who believe" is His resurrection power. He wants you to know about "His mighty power which He worked in Christ when He raised Him from the dead" right now. He wants your understanding to be enlightened, or lit up, by the resurrection power of the Lord Jesus Christ. Then, when a viper grabs hold of your life, you can shake it off and march on to fulfill your divine destiny.

Resurrection Life Enlightens You

Children of Light

But you are a chosen generation, a royal priesthood, a holy nation, His own special people, that you may proclaim the praises of Him who called you out of darkness into His marvelous light.

1 Peter 2:9

When you were born again, you were delivered out of darkness, the kingdom of darkness, which is Satan's kingdom. He is the prince of darkness. In Genesis 1:2, it says that darkness covered the earth, which can only mean that Satan had done some real damage to the perfect planet God had originally created, because we know that everything God creates is beautiful and good. Verse 2 of Genesis 1 implies that Satan's kingdom of darkness was holding the earth captive, but it also says that the Holy Spirit was "hovering over the face of the waters," just waiting for God to say the Word.

What follows in Genesis 1:3 is a perfect demonstration of resurrection life now. God spoke His Word and the Holy Spirit breathed life into the earth. At that moment, the whole planet came alive again. We always concentrate on the physical part of those six days of creation, but the basis for all of the physical, tangible transformation of the earth was spiritual illumination.

The first thing God said was, "Let there be light," and He wasn't talking about a physical light. He didn't create the sun until verse 16. In verse 3, He was talking about a spiritual light that would purge and cleanse the entire earth of the spiritual darkness of Satan that was covering it—and that light was the power of the Holy Spirit.

Resurrection life, which is the same Spirit that raised Jesus from the dead, also brings dead things to life spiritually. He purges and cleanses us and the world around us of all spiritual darkness. We have been delivered out of the dominion of darkness into God's marvelous light. We are no longer held by spiritual darkness; we are now filled with spiritual light as living spirits of God. We are enlightened through the resurrection life inside us.

I am always trying to figure out what Adam and Eve had that they lost in the fall because in our Lord Jesus Christ we got it back. I believe they functioned perfectly in every area, especially in their minds. I believe they were fully educated by the Father. They were not ignorant, because ignorance is darkness, and there is no darkness in God the Creator. No creature created in His image could be in darkness. Human beings were created with enlightened minds.

When he sinned, Adam was cut off from the life and light of God, and he became ignorant and full of dark ideas. Representing the whole human race, he lost the spiritual light that showed us the way to live.

What Is Spiritual Light?

This is the message which we have heard from Him and declare to you, that God is light and in Him is no darkness at all. If we say that we have fellowship with Him, and walk in darkness, we lie and do not practice the truth.

1 John 1:5-6

We are children of light because our Father is light and there is no darkness in Him at all. Light is the very essence and substance of God. And as long as we stay in fellowship with Him, we stay "lit up" or enlightened.

These verses also say that walking in darkness is the same as lying and not practicing the truth. Now that sounds familiar too! Jesus said He was the way, the truth, and the life in John 14:6, so spiritual light also means truth. When God said, "Let there be light," He was proclaiming the truth over the earth as the Holy Spirit brought His presence into it. The light of God's truth dispelled the darkness of ignorance and deception, which was causing the physical darkness.

As children of the God of light, we must always live in His presence and walk in His truth.

If we walk in the light as He is in the light, we have fellowship with one another, and the blood of Jesus Christ His Son cleanses us from all sin.

If we say that we have no sin, we deceive ourselves, and the truth is not in us. If we confess our sins, He is faithful and just to forgive us our sins and to cleanse us from all unrighteousness.

1 John 1:7-9

We cannot walk in the light unless we are walking with Him because God is light and Jesus is truth! When we live our lives wrapped up in God and His ways, we will keep ourselves spiritually enlightened and free of darkness.

Walking in the light is the same thing as walking in God's truth, and when we walk in the truth, the blood of Jesus Christ continually cleanses us from the effects of all our sins: past, present, and future. Now if we realize we have sinned and don't acknowledge it, if we make excuses, blame others, or refuse to take a good look at our faults and failings, then we are not walking in truth. We have stopped fellowshipping with God and have stepped out of His light. That is not a good place to be! There is no more miserable human being on the face of the earth than a Christian who has stepped away from fellowship with the Father, out of the light into darkness, by sinning.

Resurrection Life Now!

You see, Beloved, you were enlightened by the Holy Spirit on the inside of you from the moment you were born again. His resurrection life now influences everything you think, say, and do—always drawing you into a deeper relationship with God and a greater understanding of His truth. So when you choose to go against the truth, step out of the light, and away from fellowship with the Lord, you place yourself in a dark place, subject to the powers of darkness, ignorance, and deception.

John must have had some experience with this because the Holy Spirit used him to write (my paraphrase): "When you sin, confess it! Don't hide it or run from it. Face it head-on, get it out in the open, and your Father in Heaven is faithful to forgive you and cleanse you from every part of it." In other words, bring it out into the open. Get back in the light!

Spiritual light is the essence of God and His truth. He wants us to stay free by living in the light of His presence and truth. And it is His resurrection life that enlightens us so that we can live our lives to the fullest.

True Freedom

"If you abide in My word, you are My disciples indeed. And you shall know the truth, and the truth shall make you free."

John 8:31-32

Light. Truth. Freedom. They go together. They are the same, and you can't have one without the others. God is light, truth, and freedom. Jesus said that real freedom exists on the inside of you as you abide or live in His Word. His Word and His truth are the same, and the truth will unlock whatever has been holding you back. It will release you from ungodly traditions and thinking of the past. It will expose the foolishness of "old wives tales" and superstitious nonsense that has kept you bound in fear, frustration, anger, jealousy, strife, gossip—you name it. The truth of God's Word will set you free!

Resurrection Life Enlightens You

When I was about eighteen, a little after I had received the gift of the Holy Spirit, my aunt took me to a huge tent revival between Dallas and Fort Worth. A man named O. L. Jaggers ministered at an afternoon service. As I sat on that folding chair, my feet deep in sawdust, this man told us to turn to the first chapter of Ephesians. Then he started reading it out loud, verse by verse. He did not preach or teach; he just read the Bible.

I probably cannot express in words the electrifying effect just reading the Word of God had on me and everyone in that meeting. People began to shout and praise God. Periodically, we would erupt in powerful worship. There was such a spirit of revelation in that place, and the words he read were just what the book of Hebrews says they are:

> For the word of God is living and powerful, and sharper than any two-edged sword, piercing even to the division of soul and spirit, and of joints and marrow, and is a discerner of the thoughts and intents of the heart.
>
> *Hebrews 4:12*

O. L. Jaggers would read and our hearts were pierced! We had to shout and praise God. He would wait until we quieted down, then he would read some more until we couldn't hold back the expression of joy any longer. We couldn't hold back because we were being enlightened by the resurrection life, truth, and light in the Word of God. Our minds and souls were being made alive and anew by the Holy Scriptures, and we had never experienced such freedom!

You may have been afraid to step into the ministry God has called you to do. Maybe you have been so jealous of someone in your life that that's all you think about, and for years you have not done anything you were really supposed to do for the Lord. Or perhaps you find yourself continuously wrapped up in phone conversations, texting, twittering, or on other social networks that waste your time in gossip, obsessing about other people's lives. You need to get into God's Word and be set free! Read it out loud and let the light of His resurrection life enlighten you.

Sometimes we don't know where to go or what to do in a certain situation. It is like we are stuck in a dark room and are trying to feel our way out of it. What do we need? Spiritual light!

Your word is a lamp to my feet and a light to my path.

Psalm 119:105

The Word of God will literally shine His heavenly light on the path you are to take in life. I can't tell you how many times I have faced a problem, a difficult set of circumstances, or a disagreement with another person, and I felt like the enemy had me bound up in a cage of darkness and confusion. Yet all I had to do was open my Bible and read. Sometimes the Holy Spirit would tell me which passage to read; other times, just reading the first page I came to was all I needed to "see" again.

Then there have been many times when the Holy Spirit simply brought a scripture to my mind, and when I latched onto it, the lights went on! I knew it would be okay. I saw the truth. I was free of the darkness that had tried to stop me from moving forward, and God's will and way were clear. I knew where I needed to go and what I needed to do. I may not have understood it all, but I was sure of my path.

One evening I was walking my dogs and just felt led to go a different way. I started zigzagging. I thought, *Why am I walking so crazy?* This was not my usual pattern. At one point, I cut across the street and started to walk by a well-known restaurant that had an outside area where people could sit and eat. As I passed, I noticed there was only one couple sitting there. I had almost passed them when the lady said, "What pretty dogs."

That stopped me! I love to show off my dogs. I said, "This one's Toby. He's my baby. He's three years old. And this old man is Dusty. He's about twelve years old."

She stared at me and said, "Your voice. Are you Anne Gimenez?"

I said, "Yes."

She said, "You have no idea how many people in this city you have blessed. You bless us with your TV program on Sunday mornings. You have no idea." I thanked her and she went on to say, "I've been praying about a church to go to, and for several days I've been thinking about Rock Church. Now you walk right over to me! I will be there Sunday morning. I will."

You know what I did? I reached over and said, "Give me your hand." Right there in front of God and everybody else I just grabbed her hand and started praying for her. Tears came to her eyes. She said, "I will be there, you'll see me Sunday morning."

What "possessed" me to go by that restaurant instead of my usual way? The resurrection life of God inside me! He lit me up with His plan, and even though I didn't understand it, I followed the path He showed me. As a result, I got blessed and that couple got blessed. That is the power of being enlightened.

Light. Truth. Freedom in God's Word. These are the substance and strength of the resurrection life we have been given. And when we live as enlightened human beings, God can do amazing things in us, for us, with us, and through us. Now that's true freedom!

Resurrection Life Now!

The Spirit of Liberty

Nevertheless when one turns to the Lord, the veil is taken away.
Now the Lord is the Spirit; and where the Spirit of the Lord is,
there is liberty. But we all, with unveiled face, beholding as in
a mirror the glory of the Lord, are being transformed into the
same image from glory to glory, just as by the Spirit of the Lord.

2 Corinthians 3:16-18

What happens when you have a veil over your eyes? Can you see anything? Are you in darkness? Do you have any idea where you are, what you are doing, or where you are going? This is how we are before we give our lives to Jesus Christ. We live in darkness. At best, everything is cloudy and unclear. But then He—the Light of the World— saves us from our sins, the Father of Light forgives us and makes us His child, and the Holy Spirit comes to enlighten us. The veil of darkness falls from our eyes and we see the light of God's truth. We can understand His Word and the reality of our situation through a heavenly perspective instead of a human, earthly view.

The Spirit of God comes to live in our spirits and the lights go on inside us. We are enlightened! And that is the moment when we are liberated from darkness. Wherever the Spirit of the Lord abides and is given rule, there is liberty. There is so much talk today about liberty and freedom, but I think you and I can see from what is going on in the world that the only liberty and freedom we can always count on is not going to come from any government or manmade institution; permanent liberty and freedom come only from the resurrection life inside us.

God treats liberty and freedom in a different way than human beings do, however. His liberty and freedom, the resurrection life inside us, brings a responsibility with it. We are now free to grow and mature in the things of God, to become more like Jesus each day, and to serve and worship Him alone. The Spirit of God has not moved into us just to sit and be quiet! He is there to redecorate and recalibrate our lives.

Think about this: When Moses asked Pharaoh to let God's people go, when he fought for their liberty, what did he really say?

So Moses and Aaron came in to Pharaoh and said to him, "Thus says the LORD God of the Hebrews: 'How long will you refuse to humble yourself before Me? Let My people go, that they may serve Me.'"

Exodus 10:3

Moses and Aaron didn't ask for liberty just so the children of Israel could live a life of pleasure without purpose. No! The God of the Hebrews spoke through them, saying, "Let My people go, that they may serve Me." Our liberty is the privilege and ability to serve the Lord and bring glory to His name. And we can't do that without growing up in Him and being enlightened by the Holy Spirit.

If you look again at 2 Corinthians 3:16-18, you will see that when the veil comes off, you can see yourself in the mirror—and not just any mirror. This is the mirror of God's Word. You look into the truth of the Word of God, and the Spirit of God will begin to enlighten you about yourself: your gifts and callings, your strengths and weaknesses, and your hopes and fears. When you are in the light, you can see the truth. God's Word enlightens and confronts you, and you have the liberty of the Spirit to CHANGE.

Have you noticed that nothing ever stays the same? If you look up at the sky for five minutes, it will change every second. Life is just like that, and so is our resurrection life in the Lord Jesus Christ. Our flesh wants to get things in place, the way we like it, and stay there. We never want the wind to blow, the clouds to come, or the storms to pass through. We want sunshine and roses every day. But the weather changes, and so must we.

You hear people say, "This too shall pass." They say that because nothing stays the same. I thank God it doesn't because that means you and I are changing. What are we changing into? The Spirit and the Word are changing us into the image and likeness of Christ Jesus. We are growing into maturity, which means Christ is being formed in us. When He is fully formed in us, we will be a perfect expression of Him in every area of our lives.

What would spiritual maturity mean to you on a daily basis? Well, if Christ was fully formed in you, you would be enlightened, possessing His wisdom and knowledge. You would have His level of discernment. In that state of enlightenment, you would repulse sin and resist temptation the way He did. You would walk in all the gifts and fruit of the Spirit at the same time.

You say, "That's not possible." It's possible, but to get to that place, you have to change, and change is not always easy. In fact, I have found it to be painful at times. But when I would "take my liberty" and choose to follow the Spirit's leading in the light of what He was showing me, I never regretted it. Why? My soul was transformed.

Soul Transformation

You may think I am harping on this, and I am: The centerpiece of our salvation is the resurrection. What did the apostles in the Bible preach? The resurrection of Jesus Christ. Over and over the Bible tells us they preached Jesus and the resurrection. If there was no resurrection, Jesus wouldn't be any different from any other god that anybody else is worshipping, and Christians wouldn't act any different from Muslims, Hindus, or Buddhists.

Resurrection Life Enlightens You

What I'm saying is that Christians ought to be different. We are not a "try to fit in with the world" club! We are a "chosen generation, a royal priesthood, a holy nation, His own special people" (1 Peter 2:9). The King James Version says we are a "peculiar people." That says to me that we are supposed to think, speak, and act differently than the world does. We are supposed to live like we are chosen of God, royal servants of the Lord, a holy nation. Most of all, if we are peculiar, it is because we don't glorify ourselves; we love, serve, praise, and glorify the Lord.

Too many believers look and act just like the world today. They are not living like enlightened human beings. There is no outward evidence of the light and truth of resurrection life inside them. They are choosing to conform themselves to the world instead of being transformed by the Spirit and Word of God. Frankly, I just shake my head at some Christians I meet. They tell me they are believers, but their words and actions don't demonstrate it. They look and sound just like the lost souls in the world. At that point I can only pray and believe God is working in their lives, that He sees something I don't see and knows things I don't know.

If this is a grievous thing to me, a pastor, then how much more grievous is it to our Heavenly Father? He sacrificed His Son so that we could be enlightened—filled with the light of truth and set free in the liberty of His indwelling Spirit—and then He sees no change in the way some of us conduct our lives. Again, if we are enlightened, we ought to act like it! But this does not happen without submitting our souls (mind, emotions, and will) to the transforming power of the light of God's Word and the power of His Spirit.

There is therefore now no condemnation to those who are in Christ Jesus, who do not walk according to the flesh, but according to the Spirit. For the law of the Spirit of life in Christ Jesus has made me free from the law of sin and death.

Romans 8:1-2

Resurrection Life Now!

Paul is addressing Christians, those who are in Christ Jesus. He says that if we walk according to the flesh—do what we feel like doing instead of what we know God wants us to do or act like the world instead of like Jesus—we are acting like nothing has changed at the new birth. We are still operating under the law of sin and death. Furthermore, he says that if we walk in the flesh, we place ourselves under condemnation. We will not be free. We will be living under the influence of the kingdom of darkness, which operates under the law of sin and death and condemnation and shame.

On the other hand, if we choose to live by the Spirit, we will we be free of condemnation. We will walk in the light, truth, and liberty of fellowship with the Lord, under the "law of the Spirit of life in Christ Jesus." We won't live like the world lives, in fear and in bondage to all kinds of evil emotions and thoughts. We will live in a spiritual dimension where the resurrection life inside us enlightens us, bringing new life, light, and liberty to our minds and emotions. In that state of mind and heart, it will be easier make right decisions.

Let's go on in chapter 8 of Romans:

For those who live according to the flesh set their minds on the things of the flesh, but those who live according to the Spirit, the things of the Spirit. For to be carnally minded is death, but to be spiritually minded is life and peace.

Romans 8:5-6

I don't know about you, but I will choose life and peace over death any day of the week! However, the only way I can do that is to set my mind on the Spirit, to live from the resurrection life inside me instead of the old sinful desires of my flesh, the temptations of the devil, or the seductions and deceptions of the world. The only way I can live as an enlightened, spiritual, free human being is to set my mind on the Spirit.

Resurrection Life Enlightens You

By now you may be asking, "Okay. This sounds great. I want to live in light and truth and all that. I want my soul to be transformed. But please translate that into the details of my daily life. Make it real."

Spirit, Soul, and Body

Being born again is a spiritual experience. Did you notice when you got born again, you didn't change on the outside? Say you got saved at a Sunday evening service at your friend's church. The next morning you looked in the mirror and all your facial features were the same. You hadn't lost any weight. Nothing in your appearance was different, except maybe your smile was a little brighter and your heart felt lighter. Although some people are healed when they are saved, most of us are physically unchanged.

Then you went to work and everything that could go wrong went wrong. Out of your mouth came something you had said all your life, but this time you heard yourself in a whole new way. You realized something else besides your body didn't change when you were born again: your soul.

Your soul is your mind, your emotions, and your will. This is where you make all your decisions. You decide what you're going to think, what you're going to believe, what you're going to say, and how you're going to act. It is also where you deal with all kinds of negative feelings like fear, jealousy, anger, and bitterness.

The only thing you know has changed dramatically since you got saved is your spirit. When you looked in the mirror, you saw yourself through different eyes. When you made that statement at work, you heard yourself differently. That is because your spirit was alive to God and you were enlightened. You saw your life and the world around you through His eyes of truth.

Resurrection Life Now!

When you were born again, the Holy Spirit made your dead spirit alive to God. He, the bearer of resurrection life, also came to live in your brand-new spirit. So it is in your spirit that you are connected to and communicate with God. However, your soul and your body are a different story.

The Bible says your body will not be fully "saved" and free from sin and death until the resurrection.

Behold, I tell you a mystery: We shall not all sleep, but we shall all be changed — in a moment, in the twinkling of an eye, at the last trumpet. For the trumpet will sound, and the dead will be raised incorruptible, and we shall be changed. For this corruptible must put on incorruption, and this mortal must put on immortality. So when this corruptible has put on incorruption, and this mortal has put on immortality, then shall be brought to pass the saying that is written: "Death is swallowed up in victory."

1 Corinthians 15:51-54

Until we rise to meet Jesus in the air and our physical bodies are completely rid of all desire to sin, you have to deal with your flesh. You still have the carnal nature, which desires to sin, in your physical body. The Good News is that your spirit is now alive to God and possesses the resurrection life of the Spirit to overcome any sinful tendency or temptation of your flesh. That's where your soul comes in.

Your soul is where the battle takes place, because your mind, emotions, and will determine what you will think, say, and do. To stop thinking, speaking, and acting like an unsaved sinner, and to start thinking, speaking, and acting like Jesus, your soul needs to be transformed and learn to obey the Spirit in your spirit instead of your carnal, sinful flesh. How do you do that? You have to go to war!

Resurrection Life Enlightens You

For though we walk in the flesh, we do not war according to the flesh. For the weapons of our warfare are not carnal but mighty in God for pulling down strongholds, casting down arguments and every high thing that exalts itself against the knowledge of God, bringing every thought into captivity to the obedience of Christ, and being ready to punish all disobedience when your obedience is fulfilled.

2 Corinthians 10:3-6

You have to bring every thought into submission to Christ. That's the beginning of real change in your life. You have to fight to do that, because your flesh will fight for what it wants, but your soul calls the shots. The soul is the part of you that's between your spirit and your body. In your soul, you choose either to obey God or the devil, to live by the Spirit or your selfish flesh. That's why the Scriptures say that the battlefield is in your mind.

Your Mind Is the Key

And do not be conformed to this world, but be transformed by the renewing of your mind, that you may prove what is that good and acceptable and perfect will of God.

Romans 12:2

In the Greek text, the word translated "transformed" is *metamorphoo*. Does that look familiar? The English word "metamorphosis" comes from this word. Metamorphoo means: "To transform, transfigure, change one's form.... In Rom 12:2 and 2 Cor. 3:18, the idea of transformation refers to an invisible process in Christians which takes place or begins to take place during their life in this age."[1]

The process of transformation is invisible because it takes place in your mind. You fight all of your battles in your mind. Then, when you win those battles and are transformed, people will see it in your life. You will speak and act like Jesus. They will see His resurrection life in you. This happens because your thoughts are on the Lord and aligned with His truth.

On the other hand, if Satan can get you to entertain thoughts of discouragement—telling you people are talking about you, doing you wrong, and nobody loves you or appreciates you—he can defeat you. He can bring you down to such a low point that if you don't kill yourself, he will make you sick unto death. But there's only one reason he is able to do that: You have forgotten that you are born of the Spirit, that you have resurrection life in you and are enlightened. Romans 8:11 says that the same Spirit that raised Jesus from the dead lives inside your spirit, and if you let Him, He will bring resurrection life to your soul.

How do you do that? The Bible says that you need to "renew" your mind, to make it "new." How do you do that? Grow in the knowledge of God by reading, studying, and meditating in God's Word. Turn on the lights! God's Word will alter your thinking so that you can choose to live a resurrection life right now instead of living out of that mess you made ten years ago. You can choose to forgive instead of becoming bitter. You can choose not to indulge your flesh and instead worship the Lord by carrying out His will.

The entrance of Your words gives light; It gives understanding to the simple.

Psalm 119:130

When your mind is full of God's Word, resurrection life will flow from your spirit to your soul and enlighten your natural mind with the mind of Christ. It will bring forth creative thoughts. It will settle your emotions and purge your heart of any bad attitudes. All this happens when you renew your mind with the Word of God.

Another important key to being transformed is praying in the Spirit, in your heavenly language. The Bible says you are building yourself up in your most holy faith (Jude 1:20), and faith dispels fear because light dispels darkness. Doubt and unbelief fall by the wayside when you march on in faith. Faith also gives you the ability to say no to temptation and trust God for something better. Something better always includes a mind and heart that have chosen God's way over the selfish, worldly, evil way—and so you become more like Jesus.

Fight, Fight, Fight!

I will tell you the truth, you are going to have to fight for this! You are probably going to have to change some of your habits, your lifestyle, and maybe even your friends. Why? Sometimes we have to do things differently and stop being around certain people in order to give the resurrection life inside us a chance to change our thinking. We can't be enlightened if we are continually around the darkness we used to walk in. We have to refocus our lives on the Word and the Spirit. We have to "eat" different spiritual food. Like physical food that is nutritious and delicious, the spiritual food of prayer and the Word will make your soul healthy and strong—enlightened to know the "good and acceptable and perfect will of God" (Romans 12:2).

The Bible tells us in 2 Corinthians 10:3-6 above to bring "every thought into captivity to the obedience of Christ, and being ready to punish all disobedience when your obedience is fulfilled." The Message puts it this way:

> The world is unprincipled. It's dog-eat-dog out there! The world doesn't fight fair. But we don't live or fight our battles that way—never have and never will. The tools of our trade aren't for mar-

keting or manipulation, but they are for demolishing that entire massively corrupt culture. We use our powerful God-tools for smashing warped philosophies, tearing down barriers erected against the truth of God, fitting every loose thought and emotion and impulse into the structure of life shaped by Christ. Our tools are ready at hand for clearing the ground of every obstruction and building lives of obedience into maturity.

Do you see the fight in this? If you want your soul to be transformed, you have to censor your thoughts, because that is where everything you say and do begins. Whether you speak God's truth in love or commit a crime, it starts with a thought.

Let me tell you something that is so important for you to know to fight this battle of the mind and win. The enemy cannot get to your spirit because that is where the Holy Spirit resides, but he can introduce all kinds of thoughts and ideas to your mind. Your natural mind is the door for the devil and his demonic forces. He knows that he can influence and control you if he can capture your thoughts. So your battles are fought—and won or lost—in your mind.

Remember how the serpent tempted Eve? He said in Genesis 3:1 (my paraphrase), "Now really, did God say you couldn't eat the fruit of every tree in this garden? Look at this one, the tree of the knowledge of good and evil. Doesn't the fruit look delicious? Why would a loving God ever deprive you of anything that looked that good?"

You have to guard the doorway of your eyes and your ears. What you see and what you hear can deceive you and mislead you. There are times you have to get up and walk away. Sometimes you just have to turn the TV off, throw the book in the trash, or walk out of the theater. If anyone asks you about it, you can say, "I just don't want to think or talk or act like that. I don't want my life to look like that in any way."

Resurrection Life Enlightens You

The Word says that to be carnally minded is death, but to be spiritually minded is life and peace. If you've got the Holy Spirit on the inside of you, that's resurrection life, and His desire is to bring all the dead things in your mind, emotions, and will alive spiritually. He wants to resurrect your soul and make you alive to God in your thoughts, your emotions, and every decision. He wants to enlighten you!

What Happens If You Choose Darkness?

It's your choice. God cannot force you to fight the good fight of faith in your mind. You can go after the lusts of your flesh, give in to all ungodly appetites, and satisfy every carnal desire. If you choose this way, everything you see, taste, feel, smell, or hear—no matter how sinful—you will do. You will constantly think about things you know do not please God, and then you will find yourself doing things you never thought you would do. You will sink lower and lower, and the condemnation will become heavier and heavier.

This is why Christians who do not choose to live from the resurrection life inside them, by the Spirit and according to the Word, are the most miserable people on Earth. They are more beaten down and discouraged than the most sinful unbeliever because the Spirit of God inside them is continually reminding them that they are living way below their spiritual position. They are settling for so much less! Spiritually they are seated with Jesus in Heaven, but they are refusing to fight the battle in their mind. So they live a sinful, carnal life of darkness. They are not where they are supposed to be.

> *The mind set on the flesh is hostile toward God; for it does not subject itself to the law of God, for it is not even able to do so, and those who are in the flesh cannot please God.*
>
> *Romans 8:7-8 NASB*

These people can't please God because they choose to think thoughts that are against the will and the Word of God. They were created to please God and enjoy His company, but because they are entertaining all kinds of fleshly thoughts and ideas that are hostile to God, they are separating themselves from Him and not pleasing themselves either.

For a while, Christians can deceive themselves into believing they are doing okay in sin and not living for God, but eventually the rotten fruit of their darkness and deception will manifest. It will be obvious to them and to everyone around them that they are far from the Lord—out of fellowship and out of the light and truth that bring life and liberty.

The person I just described will wake up on Sunday morning, and the battle in their mind commences. They look at the clock, know it's time to get up and go to church, and make a series of decisions. They can turn their thoughts to the things of God, pray in the Spirit to build their faith, open their Bible or meditate on Scripture; and the Holy Spirit will bring their soul to resurrection life, so they can rise up to fellowship with the Lord, the Church, and receive the encouragement and further enlightenment God wants to give them.

Or, they can turn their thoughts to more sleep, watching television, playing their favorite sport, and eating and drinking whatever they want. They will mentally walk away from the light that calls to them from within and move into darkness. They will reject the resurrection life inside them and refuse to be made alive in their soul by the Light of their spirit.

That's why we also need to stay in fellowship with other believers, who will help us to keep our minds on the Lord and do the right thing. Remember the story about the mother who told her son, "You've got to get up and go to church."

He said, "I'm not going to church."

She said, "Give me two reasons."

He said, "Number one, I don't like those people, and number two, they don't like me. Now you give me one reason why I should go."

She said, "Well, you're the pastor."

Sometimes even pastors forget how powerful their thoughts can be! Recently I read that each thought produces an emotion. Whatever you are thinking right now will cause an emotional response that releases a chemical in your body. Every time you think a bad thought, a wrong thought, an incorrect thought, an angry thought, a mad thought, or a lustful thought, you're releasing a chemical in your body that affects your overall well-being in a negative way. What you think can even make you physically sick or mentally ill.

On the other hand, what you think can also make you well and give you strength, wisdom, and courage. That's why God told Joshua to meditate in the Word day and night (Joshua 1:8). By keeping his mind on the truth of God's Word, Joshua stayed enlightened. He was able to take the Promised Land because he first won the battle in his mind. He did not choose darkness. He chose to be enlightened.

Be a Living Sacrifice

Don't refuse to be enlightened in your soul!

Reject all ungodly thoughts and choose to think like God, meditating on His Word. You can use your imagination and be creative. In fact, when you stay in the Spirit and win the battle of your mind, you will discover all kinds of exciting things. Remember, God says in 3 John 2 that you will prosper in every area of your life "as your soul prospers."

Resurrection Life Now!

Today we must hold to the resurrection of Jesus Christ more than ever before. Paul said,

> *I beseech you therefore brethren, by the mercies of God, to make yourself a living sacrifice, wholly acceptable to God, which is your reasonable service.*

> *Romans 12:1*

When Jesus died on the cross, God was fully satisfied. Jesus was the last dead sacrifice, and then He was resurrected to live forever with His Father. Now, everyone who follows Him is a living sacrifice. We give Him our whole heart and lay down our lives for Him because He is resurrected and in Him, so are we. This is our reasonable service because He has filled us with resurrection life and enlightened us. He shows us the truth and sets us free continually.

Paul said,

> *But what things were gain to me, these I have counted loss for Christ. Yet indeed I also count all things loss for the excellence of the knowledge of Christ Jesus my Lord, for whom I have suffered the loss of all things, and count them as rubbish, that I may gain Christ and be found in Him.*

> *Philippians 3:7-9*

We cry over the things we have to lay aside for Jesus, when we ought to be celebrating the fact that in His wisdom and strength we can! We weep and mourn and feel so sorry for ourselves sometimes. And I'm talking about myself! But you know something, I bet no one (in the American church at least) has ever lost everything for Jesus. There are few believers like Paul in this world, but I want to be one! For what we gain when we really put every step we take in His hands is a life that is holy, pure, undefiled—and a witness of the resurrection power of the Lord Jesus Christ to everyone around us.

When your mind is fully immersed in the resurrection life of the mind of Christ, then you are going to speak the right thing at the right time, you are going to do the right thing at the right time, and God will see to it that you will be at the right place at the right time—to be blessed and to be a blessing.

> *Jesus spoke to them again, saying, "I am the light of the world. He who follows Me shall not walk in darkness, but have the light of life.*

> *John 8:12*

> *I have come as a light into the world, that whoever believes in Me should not abide in darkness.*

> *John 12:46*

Jesus said He was the light of the world, and in Matthew 5:14, He told us that we were the light of the world. If we abide in Him, we will live in the light of His truth, which sets us free to love, live for, and serve Him and His people.

My prayer is that when you and I walk into a room, people who are sitting in darkness will see the great light of resurrection life in us and yearn for that life and light in themselves.

> *"The people who sat in darkness have seen a great light, and upon those who sat in the region and shadow of death*

> *Light has dawned."*

> *Matthew 4:16*

Resurrection Life Now!

Chapter 7

Resurrection Life Quickens You

And the LORD God commanded the man, saying, "Of every tree
of the garden you may freely eat; but of the tree of the knowledge
of good and evil you shall not eat, for in the day that you eat of
it you shall surely die."

Genesis 2:16-17

Adam sinned. God had said (literally), "Don't eat of the tree of the
knowledge of good and evil, or you will die twice, first spiritually and
then physically." Adam disobeyed Him, and he and the whole human
race were immediately separated from God spiritually. We are spiritually dead and eventually become physically dead because all life begins
and ends in the presence of God. We became vulnerable to sickness,
disease, and death. We went from immortality to mortality through
the sin of one man. But God had a plan for us!

For the wages of sin is death, but the gift of God is eternal life in
Christ Jesus our Lord.

Romans 6:23

God never created us to die. He created us to live. Sickness and disease are not His will for humanity. He created us to be well and whole

in every area of our being. When Adam severed our relationship with God through sin, he also brought sickness and disease into our lives. So God the Father, in His infinite love and mercy, sent His Son Jesus to pay the debt for the sin that caused our spiritual and physical death. Jesus said, "I have come that they may have life, and that they may have it more abundantly" (John 10:10). Abundant life means first being restored spiritually to God through eternal life. Then, as a result of having eternal life, we also have resurrection life now, making all dead and dying things alive—including our physical bodies.

> But if the Spirit of him that raised up Jesus from the dead dwell in you, he that raised up Christ from the dead shall also quicken your mortal bodies by his Spirit that dwelleth in you.
>
> *Romans 8:11 KJV*

"Quicken" is a great word. It depicts the Holy Spirit, living in your spirit, breathing life into every cell of your physical body, making all dead things come alive. Resurrection life is more powerful than all the vitamins, minerals, herbs, and nutritious food you could eat to make your body healthy and strong. Those things are wonderful, and I believe you are to take good care of your body because it is "the temple of the Holy Spirit," (1 Corinthians 6:19); but when you are weak and sick in your physical body, and all else fails, the resurrection life inside you will quicken you.

No one knows this better than I do. It wasn't that long ago when no medical treatment was working and I almost died. I was at a retreat for our pastors in Florida, doing what God called me to do, and I felt no pain or discomfort. All of a sudden I collapsed, and my daughter Robin took me to my cousin's to rest. After a little while I said to my daughter, "Go get your daddy."

John had been gone two years, so she said, "Well Mother, Daddy's not here."

Resurrection Life Quickens You

I said, "Yes, he is. He just went down the hallway." Then I thought a minute and said, "Robin, if I'm seeing the dead, I'm in trouble."

That's when they knew I needed medical attention, and they rushed me to the hospital. By the time I got there I was unconscious. They had to get my heart started with the paddles, and they had all kinds of tubes in me. The doctor pulled Robin aside and said, "You better prepare yourself. Your mother will not live through the night."

She said, "You don't know my mother. She will live."

I lapsed into a coma and remained that way for fifteen days. I was hooked up to all kinds of machines and on life support. My heart was functioning at only 10 percent. My kidneys and liver had shut down. I was on a breathing machine. Every night they told Robin I was going to die.

One day a doctor came in to see me and said, "No one comes back from this kind of thing."

Robin had had enough. She told the doctor to step out of my room and said, "You see that line right there on the threshold? Don't you ever step over that again. I will not have you in my mother's room saying she's going to die. She can hear you, and I'm not going to let you say that." Then she went to the nurses and said, "I want to know who the head doctor is."

They said, "You were just talking to him."

They called her the troublemaker from that day! She requested that a Christian doctor, Dr. Crandall, come in to see me. By the time Dr. Crandall examined me, I was coming out of the coma. He said, "She will not die. She will live." Then Robin decided to move me to Dallas Presbyterian Hospital, where I could be treated by a heart specialist she had heard about.

They flew me to Dallas, where they did every test imaginable for two days. I was pretty fuzzy during that time, but one night I remember a team of doctors coming in to see me. One of them leaned over, looked at me, and said, "My God, woman. Eat. You have been pushed to the brink of starvation."

For the fifteen days I had been in Florida, they had given me fluids only. They thought I was going to die anyway, so they didn't feed me anything. When I finally woke up, I was not sure where I was or why I was there. I didn't know what had happened to me. I thought I might be hallucinating about being in a hospital. I thought it was a dream. Then I realized I couldn't move. One of the first things I said was, "Robin, am I paralyzed?"

"Mother, you're not paralyzed. Why do you ask that?"

I said, "Because all I can do is turn my head."

After fifteen days of not moving, no nourishment, and not being turned in my bed or being massaged, my muscles had atrophied. I had lost all muscle strength. Even after I was awake, they would put food in front of me, but I couldn't get to it. I had no strength to feed myself. As soon as the doctor realized I was starving, the nurses and Robin began to help me.

As I regained some physical strength, the heart doctor decided to put me on some blood pressure medicine, and after two days I could hardly wake up. Robin got me to another heart specialist, who had a machine that scanned my heart to see everything that was going on with it. He said, "I can see everything an autopsy would show. When this chamber is vibrating, you've had a stroke. When this chamber is vibrating, you've had a heart attack. When all four of them are vibrating, a virus has attacked your heart. In your case, all four are vibrating."

Resurrection Life Quickens You

This doctor was the first one to diagnose me correctly, and he immediately took me off the blood pressure medicine. Later he said to Robin, "Three more days and you wouldn't have been able to wake your mother up." He indicated it was because that medicine had been slowing down my heart. Because of that, my body was filled with fluid, and they had to get over fifteen pounds of fluid out of me in the next two days. I also had developed pneumonia. BUT GOD!

The devil tried to take me out by sending a rare virus to attack my heart. He forgot that I have resurrection life on the inside of me! He forgot that the Holy Spirit is living inside me, quickening and making alive everything he was trying to kill. He also forgot the power of the prayers of the saints. Robin had posted on Facebook, "My mother, Pastor Anne Gimenez, is in the hospital and is not expected to live. Please pray!" Believers all over the world responded and prayed, and so the enemy was defeated through the mighty name of our Lord Jesus Christ and the quickening power of the Holy Spirit in me.

The months that followed were very hard. I had to learn to walk again, and if you've never been there, I hope you'll never know what it's like. I cried when I couldn't get up, and they would raise me up like a ragdoll. They would tell me to stand, but I had no strength in my body.

After about a week, I looked down at my numb, useless legs, and heard in my spirit, "She will not die. She will live and preach My gospel."

That was the quickening power of the Holy Spirit!

That was the resurrection life of Jesus making my physical body come alive!

With this word from the Lord, I continued to recover.

Resurrection Life Now!

Know the Time

God's Word is true and His promises are "Yea and amen" to everyone who believes. Robin knew that Jesus was the resurrection and the life for Lazarus, and He was the resurrection and the life for me. So that's how she dealt with my illness. But let me just say that you cannot take this to a foolish extreme. Yes, Jesus raised Lazarus from the dead, and that same resurrection life is in you right now, but when a believer's time to go to Heaven arrives, that is between them and God. You may not be able to raise them up as Jesus did Lazarus. Jesus raised Lazarus because it was God's will; it wasn't Lazarus' time to go.

Let me tell you something: The days of your life are numbered by God alone! When you gave your life to Jesus Christ, you put your life and health and well-being in His hands. You can say with the apostle Paul, "I know whom I have believed and am persuaded that He is able to keep what I have committed to Him until that Day" (2 Timothy 1:12). What have you committed to Him? Your entire life!

I'm not saying you won't go through battles or have to fight and struggle to stay alive. There is a devil out there who wants to kill you just like he tried to kill me, and living for Jesus Christ is hard at times. But when that demonic virus attacked my heart, God's resurrection life quickened and brought to life my dying body because it was not my time to go.

My life is secure and safe in God's hands, and He will be the One to decide when it's time for me to leave this robe of clay and head home to Heaven. Until then, I've got my high heels on, preaching in any pulpit that will have me, because I want as many as will receive Jesus Christ to have the same resurrection life that's in me.

When my husband, Bishop John Gimenez, went to Heaven, we knew it was his time. It was hard to face, but it helped to know that it was God's will and we would see him again. After awhile, when we got to thinking back to just before he died, we realized that John had been preparing for his departure. He knew his time had come.

When I got sick I had had no such warning! It was not my time and Robin knew it. I knew it. What you need to realize more than anything else is that your life in Jesus Christ is all about communing with the Holy Spirit so that you can know the will of God for your life, and sometimes the will for another person's life. Robin was communing with the Holy Spirit in that hospital, and when the doctor said I was going to die, her spirit recoiled. Her mind and heart were enlightened and she knew that was not the truth. So she did what she had to do to see that life was spoken over me and I got the medical help I needed. Through the faith and prayers of the saints, the resurrection life on the inside of me was released to quicken my dying body.

Just Like Paul

My situation was not unusual if we compare it to what the apostle Paul experienced. In Acts 14, there is the account of when he was actually stoned to death. Paul and Barnabas had preached the Gospel in Iconium and many Gentiles and Jews believed, but the city became divided and the unbelieving Jews began to plan to stone them. Barnabas and Paul heard about the plan and left. They went to Derbe and Lystra, where many more were saved, but the angry Jews from Iconium and Antioch followed them to Lystra.

> *Then Jews from Antioch and Iconium came there; and having persuaded the multitudes, they stoned Paul and dragged him out of the city, supposing him to be dead. However, when the disciples gathered around him, he rose up and went into the city. And the next day he departed with Barnabas to Derbe.*

> *Acts 14:19-20*

Resurrection Life Now!

When you got stoned in Paul's day, and I don't mean on marijuana, they threw rocks at you until your bones broke and your muscles were like pudding. It was a terribly painful way to die, and Paul went through this. The people who did this to him left because they thought he was dead. That was in verse 19, but then verse 20 begins with, "However." However means that there was something the people who stoned Paul didn't know, and that something was going to change the entire situation.

That something was the resurrection life on the inside of Paul! The Holy Spirit in him said, "No! It's not his time to go!" And He breathed life back into every broken bone and every wasted muscle and nerve and blood vessel. He quickened Paul's mortal body, and Paul stood up and said, "Barnabas, what are you doing just standing around here? We have to get to Derbe and get some more people saved and healed and delivered and set free!"

There is something more we need to see, though. The Bible says the disciples gathered around Paul's dead body, and because of that he got up. There was a reason the Holy Spirit could quicken Paul's dead body. The faith of those standing around Paul released the resurrection life inside them and him. They were the ones who believed Jesus was the resurrection and the life, just like my daughter Robin had, and Paul rose up totally healed.

Sometimes the doctor and the medicine will raise you up. Sometimes you just need to obey the leading of the Holy Spirit and eat the right thing and exercise and take good care of the temple where He lives, cooperating with the life inside you. But sometimes only the resurrection life inside you can raise you up.

I want to say something else about this: There is always a cooperation between the quickening power of the Holy Spirit and what you do in the natural to heal your body. When I was recovering from my illness, my doctor was amazed. I would go in every week to see him and he would do all kinds of tests. Then he would say the same thing: "Your progress is amazing. I have never seen a physical body heal so quickly and so well."

It was obvious to me why this was happening. The same Spirit who raised Jesus from the dead lives in me and was quickening and making alive my sick body. Every organ that virus had destroyed was being brought back to life. My faith, Robin's faith, and the faith of all the believers who were praying for me released the resurrection life in me to make my recovery a supernatural recovery.

Not too many months later, they had to help me back to the pulpit in our church. Then, not too many months after that, I was back in my high heels, preaching and shouting the praises of God!

Use What You Have

If you have Jesus Christ in you, you've got resurrection life on the inside of you. Use what you have! Use it not just for yourself but also for others. When Lazarus died, Jesus said to Martha, "Your brother will rise again" (John 11:23).

Martha said (my paraphrase), "Yes, I know Lazarus will rise again at the resurrection of the dead." She was thinking what a lot of believers think, that the resurrection life of Jesus Christ is only for the final resurrection of our physical bodies at the Rapture or, for some, at His Second Coming.

Jesus set her straight when He said, "I am the resurrection and the life" (John 11:25), and He meant NOW. Then He demonstrated that truth when He raised Lazarus from the dead. What does this mean for you and for me? The resurrection life on the inside of us is for right now, here in the present time. The Holy Spirit wants to quicken and make alive our bodies now. He wants to heal our children and neighbors and friends now.

You can read all kinds of books devoted to healing the sick through the power of prayer in the name of Jesus, so I'm not going to get into all the theological arguments for why physical healing is for today and how it's God's will for us to be healthy and strong. What I want you to see is a lot simpler than that. The Word of God says that the same Spirit that raised Jesus from the dead lives in you and will quicken and make alive your physical body right now!

Not only will the resurrection life of God quicken your mortal body, but you can transmit the resurrection life inside you to someone else and watch the Holy Spirit quicken their body too, just like Peter and John and so many others have done.

Now Peter and John went up together to the temple at the hour of prayer, the ninth hour. And a certain man lame from his mother's womb was carried, whom they laid daily at the gate of the temple which is called Beautiful, to ask alms from those who entered the temple; who, seeing Peter and John about to go into the temple, asked for alms. And fixing his eyes on him, with John, Peter said, "Look at us." So he gave them his attention, expecting to receive something from them.

Then Peter said, "Silver and gold I do not have, but what I do have I give you: In the name of Jesus Christ of Nazareth, rise up and walk."

And he took him by the right hand and lifted him up, and immediately his feet and ankle bones received strength. So he, leaping up, stood and walked and entered the temple with them—walking, leaping, and praising God.

Resurrection Life Quickens You

And all the people saw him walking and praising God. Then they knew that it was he who sat begging alms at the Beautiful Gate of the temple; and they were filled with wonder and amazement at what had happened to him.

Acts 3:1-10

All Peter and John wanted to do was go to the Temple and pray, but they were stopped by a man who had been lame his entire life. Everyone in town knew this man because he sat at the Temple, day after day, begging. That's how he supported himself. But Peter and John had something he needed, and it wasn't money. They said, "We don't have any money, but we will give you what we have." What did they have? The quickening power of resurrection life!

This resurrection life is stronger than any force of sickness and death that comes against us. When Peter and John commanded, "In the name of Jesus Christ of Nazareth, rise up and walk," the quickening power of the Holy Spirit poured all over that lame man's body. It made his feet and ankles so alive that all he could do was jump up and start crying, "Praise God!" This was a sign and wonder to everyone who knew that lame beggar that Jesus was alive!

Peter and John were simply using what they had, giving what they had to give, and you can too. Remember what Jesus told the disciples before He ascended to Heaven? He is saying the same thing to you today:

"Go into all the world and preach the gospel to every creature. He who believes and is baptized will be saved; but he who does not believe will be condemned. And these signs will follow those who believe: In My name they will cast out demons; they will speak with new tongues; they will take up serpents; and if they

*drink anything deadly, it will by no means hurt them; they will
lay hands on the sick, and they will recover."*

Mark 16:15-18

You will lay your hands on the sick, and they will recover. When
you place your hands on someone, your spirit hands—which are filled
with the quickening power of the Holy Spirit—will transfer resurrection life into their body. It is so simple that we miss it!

Think about this: People are terrified that someone with a cold or
the flu will touch them and they will get their sickness. We wash our
hands every five minutes and some people even wear masks to keep
from coming into contact with someone else's germs. We believe in
catching another person's disease more than we believe in catching another believer's quickening power—the resurrection life of the Spirit!

*Is anyone among you sick? Let him call for the elders of the
church, and let them pray over him, anointing him with oil in
the name of the Lord. And the prayer of faith will save the sick,
and the Lord will raise him up.*

James 5:14-15

The anointing oil represents the Holy Spirit, who quickens your
mortal body. You may or may not use the physical oil, but when you
lay your alive-with-the-quickening-power-of-God hands on a sick
person, believe they will "catch" the divine healing you are giving to
them. Remember, a flu bug will die because it is temporary; but the
quickening power of the Holy Spirit is permanent and forever alive in
you! You just have to believe it and use what you have.

Resurrection Life Quickens You

Snakes and Poison

In Mark 16:15-18, Jesus said you would be able to pick up snakes and drink poison, but you would not be hurt. There are some churches that bring poisonous snakes into their meetings and pick them up just to demonstrate that the Word of God is true. This is total foolishness! They have completely misunderstood what Jesus meant.

Jesus didn't mean you can go out and play with rattlesnakes and drink arsenic at your next campmeeting or dinner party! In Jesus' time they walked everywhere, and they slept on the ground when they traveled. They often ran into snakes, and Jesus said, "Look, you don't have to be afraid of anything anymore. If you come across a serpent, just pick it up and throw it out of the way. It can't hurt you because you have My resurrection life in you."

Also back in that day, the way they got rid of people was to poison their drink. This was how kings were assassinated, and that is why there were cupbearers. Cupbearers tasted the wine or drink before the king to make sure it was okay. If anybody was going to drop dead, it was going to be the cupbearer. (Not a great job to have!) So Jesus was assuring His disciples, who were already beginning to see that following Him meant having enemies who might want to kill them, that they could eat and drink without fear.

Beloved, you do not have to live your life in fear that some corporation is going to manufacture a food or drink that will have something in it that will kill you. You don't have to be afraid when God sends you on a mission into a jungle or a primitive place that snakes or wild animals are going to jump out and send you to Heaven before your time.

Whenever you doubt the quickening power of the Holy Spirit in you, whenever you need to be reminded of the keeping power of the resurrection life in you, read the truth about yourself and God:

Those who live in the shelter of the Most High will find rest in the shadow of the Almighty. This I declare about the LORD: He alone is my refuge, my place of safety; he is my God, and I trust him. For he will rescue you from every trap and protect you from deadly disease. He will cover you with his feathers. He will shelter you with his wings. His faithful promises are your armor and protection. Do not be afraid of the terrors of the night, nor the arrow that flies in the day. Do not dread the disease that stalks in darkness, nor the disaster that strikes at midday. Though a thousand fall at your side, though ten thousand are dying around you, these evils will not touch you. Just open your eyes, and see how the wicked are punished. If you make the LORD your refuge, if you make the Most High your shelter, no evil will conquer you; no plague will come near your home. For he will order his angels to protect you wherever you go. They will hold you up with their hands so you won't even hurt your foot on a stone. You will trample upon lions and cobras; you will crush fierce lions and serpents under your feet! The LORD says, "I will rescue those who love me. I will protect those who trust in my name. When they call on me, I will answer; I will be with them in trouble. I will rescue and honor them. I will reward them with a long life and give them my salvation."

Psalm 91 NLT

Your Legal Right

Most of the time, when someone needs healing, we pray and proclaim these verses of Scripture:

But He was wounded for our transgressions, He was bruised for our iniquities; The chastisement for our peace was upon Him, and by His stripes we are healed.

Isaiah 53:5

Resurrection Life Quickens You

Himself bore our sins in His own body on the tree, that we, having died to sins, might live for righteousness—by whose stripes you were healed.

1 Peter 2:24

These verses are God's Word to us and by themselves can bring healing to our lives, but I believe the Lord is leading us into a deeper understanding of our legal right to walk in a body that is completely whole and healthy. This understanding involves living a resurrection life now.

But now Christ is risen from the dead, and has become the first-fruits of those who have fallen asleep. For since by man came death, by Man also came the resurrection of the dead. For as in Adam all die, even so in Christ all shall be made alive.

1 Corinthians 15:20-22

We died in Adam, but we are "made alive" in the Lord Jesus Christ. The Greek wording here means "to cause to live, make alive, give life ... of the spirit, quickening as respects the spirit, endued with new and greater powers of life."[1] This is talking about resurrection life now!

Let's go back to the book of Romans:

The law of the Spirit of life in Christ Jesus has made me free from the law of sin and death.

Romans 8:2

What kind of life is in Christ Jesus? Eternal life and resurrection life. The law of life in Christ Jesus has made you free from the law of sin and death. In Him, you are liberated from the law of sin that causes death to rule your mortal body. When you were baptized into the body of Christ, you were baptized first into His death, when He paid the price for all your sins and satisfied God's justice on the cross. What that means is that if sin is no longer hanging over your head, then the devil has no legal right to make you sick!

> *Or do you not know that as many of us as were baptized into Christ Jesus were baptized into His death? Therefore we were buried with Him through baptism into death, that just as Christ was raised from the dead by the glory of the Father, even so we also should walk in newness of life.*
>
> *Romans 6:3-4*

You were baptized, immersed into Jesus' resurrection from the dead. You rose from the dead and went from living under the law of sin and death to living under the law of the Spirit of life in Christ Jesus. Now you live in "newness of life," according to His resurrection life in you.

You are new! When you were born from above and put into the body of Christ, a new law began working in your entire being, including your physical body. It's the law of the Spirit of life, the law of resurrection life in Christ Jesus. Every day you are new in spirit, soul, and body.

> *Now if we died with Christ, we believe that we shall also live with Him, knowing that Christ, having been raised from the dead, dies no more. Death no longer has dominion over Him.*
>
> *Romans 6:8-9*

You are in Christ Jesus, and you are one with Him. If death has no rule over Him, then it has no rule over you either! In Him you are living under a new law of resurrection life. The Holy Spirit in your spirit quickens and makes alive your physical or mortal body.

Resurrection Life Quickens You

But if the Spirit of Him who raised Jesus from the dead dwells in you, He who raised Christ from the dead will also give life to your mortal bodies through His Spirit who dwells in you.

Romans 8:11

Beloved, believe that every day you live, the Holy Spirit is quickening your mortal body, making it alive and well and healthy and strong so you can fulfill God's will for your life. Satan can't make you sick or kill you because he cannot make the Holy Spirit sick or kill the resurrection life on the inside of you! That's why John wrote: "He who is in you is greater than he who is in the world" (1 John 4:4). The Holy Spirit is greater than any sickness or disease the devil can throw at you.

Getting Through It

Living for Jesus Christ doesn't mean you will never deal with sickness or have an accident that harms your physical body. Life in Him is not without problems because you still live in a body that is not fully resurrected and contains that old desire to sin, on a planet filled with all kinds of crazy people and diseases, contending with a devil who would like to destroy you. I have a testimony not because I never was sick but because the devil tried to take me out and did not succeed. But I had to fight my way through it.

When I became conscious, I couldn't do anything but turn my head. Slowly I began to realize that if I didn't get out of that bed, I'd never preach again. And after about a month and a half I began to say to myself, "There's nothing in this bed that's going to heal me. I've got to get up. I've got to get out of it. I've got to try to walk."

I couldn't even stand up in the beginning. They would put a belt around me to lift me to my feet and say, "Now walk. Move your feet." I'd just look at my feet, and they didn't move. But I had faith and I had help. There was resurrection life in me!

Resurrection Life Now!

Yes, you will go through storms. Yes, you will have pain and suffering from time to time. But that is when God can show Himself strong in your behalf. That is when the Comforter holds you in His arms and tells you it's going to be okay.

When Jesus was about to be crucified, He wanted to prepare His disciples as much as He could. He wanted to reassure them that when He left this earth, they would not be without Him. He tried to explain to them about the Holy Spirit. He said,

> *I will pray the Father, and he shall give you another Comforter, that he may abide with you for ever;*
>
> *Even the Spirit of truth; whom the world cannot receive, because it seeth him not, neither knoweth him: but ye know him; for he dwelleth with you, and shall be in you.*
>
> *John 14:16-17 KJV*

I quoted the King James Version because it uses the word "Comforter." The New King James Version uses the word "Helper." When you are going through a terrible struggle to be healed of an illness, and when you are fighting pain, you want help, but you also need the Comforter! When I looked down at my useless legs and saw my withered body in the mirror, when it was all I could do to stand on my feet, it was the Comforter who spoke to my spirit, "She will not die. She will live and preach My gospel."

> *He sent His word and healed them, and delivered them from their destructions.*
>
> *Psalm 107:20*

When I was so discouraged about my physical condition, the word the Comforter spoke to me that day healed me! God's word to me delivered me from all the destruction the enemy had caused in my body. This Comforter is the One Jesus sent to be with you and me forever.

Resurrection Life Quickens You

You see, the kind of comfort Jesus was telling His disciples about is more than putting a warm blanket on you when you are cold. The Comforter reminds you that you have His resurrection life in you, that you are no longer ruled by sin and death, and you now live in a continuous state of newness of life, under the law of the Spirit of life in Christ Jesus. The Comforter infuses you with the ability to believe and receive what God has for you.

What Do You Need?

Did you ever notice that the apostle Paul never had a healing line? In fact, none of the apostles asked the people who needed healing to come forward for prayer when they preached and taught. Nevertheless, lots of people were healed in the New Testament, and Paul was one of them. When I realized this, that got me to seeking God and asking Him if there is something we are missing today.

I believe the Church is going to turn a corner about physical healing when believers realize they have the resurrection, making-dead-things-alive life of God on the inside of them. Like me, they will not have to beg God to touch them. They will not need the faith healer to pray for them every time they get sick or have an accident. They will know the Healer is living inside them, quickening their physical bodies. They will have an ever-present consciousness that He is giving them new life continuously. The moment anything attacks them or any evil befalls them physically, they will have great faith to call upon the Comforter to heal them and deliver them from all destruction.

Believers must understand that it doesn't matter what they inherited in their DNA, because they no longer live according to the law of sin and death that was over their ancestors. They now live under the law of the Spirit of life in Christ Jesus. And it does not matter what flu bug is going around, what new plague has hit the planet, or if their blood accidentally got mixed with the blood of someone with a deadly disease. The natural laws are made null and void by the resurrection life that is working in them right now.

By the Spirit, I'm seeing a generation of believers who know that their days and the days of every person who believes in and follows the Lord Jesus Christ are in the hands of God alone. They know that if the devil could kill them, he would right now! But there is something holding him back, something that prohibits him from having any power or control over their lives; and that something is the resurrection life of Jesus Christ that quickens them now. The miracles they need are not lost in past moves of God. They are for now.

I lived through and saw the amazing miracles of the healing evangelists of the 1940s and 1950s. One of the most remarkable was in a meeting with Brother O. L. Jaggers in Dallas. Midway through he said God told him He was going to open blind eyes. Brother Jaggers said, "If anybody here is blind, come up right now."

There was a handful of people who went up. One young man had been born without an eyeball in one eye. After Brother Jaggers prayed for him, he said, "Do you see anything?"

The young man answered, "No."

So he prayed for him again. He prayed for him about three times, each time asking, "Do you see anything?"

Every time, the answer was, "No."

Brother Jaggers said, "Go up and sit on the platform. Sit right there where everybody can see you, and don't leave the platform." So the young man sat there until the end of the service. Then Brother Jaggers told him to come down where he was. He said, "Now cover up your good eye. Do you see anything?"

The boy said, "No."

"Well, I'm going to pray for you, again." He prayed for him and then asked, "Do you see anything?"

"No."

By this time, I was wondering how Brother Jaggers could go on. It would be so hard to keep praying for somebody when nothing was happening, they were stone blind, and they didn't even have an eyeball. But Brother Jaggers kept praying.

Suddenly, the young man said, "I see spots of light." He was seeing the lights in the tent.

Brother Jaggers prayed again and then asked, "What do you see?"

He said, "I see trees." He was seeing the tent poles.

Brother Jaggers prayed some more and then asked, "How many fingers have I got up?" The boy answered correctly. He said, "Touch my nose and reach out." The boy did it.

There was something else that Brother Jaggers had done. He had asked five people to come up and watch the young man's eyes as he prayed for him. The first few times he prayed, he asked them what they saw. They said, "An empty eye socket."

But by the end he asked them, "What do you see?"

They said, "We see an eyeball forming. It's getting bigger and bigger." That was one of the first outstanding, creative miracles I ever saw, and it was a time of great excitement in the Church, but that was just a taste of what God wants to do now!

When people say to me, "Oh, you look so well," I whisper to them, "I have a secret." That hooks them! They have to know my secret. They lower their heads, their eyes are wide open, and they ask me, "Pastor Anne, what is it?"

Resurrection Life Now!

"Resurrection life."

Sometimes they don't get it right away, but when I explain how resurrection life quickened me and continues to quicken me, the light bulb goes on in them too. The same power that raised Jesus from the dead lives in them!

- The same resurrection life that brought Paul back to life after being stoned lives in them.

- The same resurrection life that flowed through Peter and James and made the lame man walk at the Gate Beautiful lives in them.

- The same resurrection life that created an eyeball in that young man's eye lives in them.

- And the same resurrection life that raised Anne Gimenez from near death lives in them too.

The whole Church hasn't got it yet, but as long as I draw breath, I will be preaching it, teaching it, and being a living example of it. Every morning I get up and say, "Thank You, Jesus, that I am filled with resurrection life, and the Holy Spirit quickens my mortal body all day and all night long."

One day, enough believers will get it, and what a day that will be! I can see it in my spirit, and I know it is coming. When we all get on that healing train, fueled by the quickening power of the resurrection life in us, what places we will go and what amazing exploits we will do!

Chapter 8

Resurrection Life Lifts You

Has anything ever just broken your heart? Have you experienced betrayal? Have people, even your brothers and sisters in the Lord, shocked you by hurting and offending you? We talk about times like these in this way:

"That really got me down."

"He put me down."

"She let me down."

There's a reason we use the word "down." We use it because we instinctively know by the Holy Spirit in us that God does not want us to be put down, let down, or to ever get down. That's why He put the same Spirit that raised Jesus from the dead in us—to raise and lift us up! In fact, when we were born again, He spiritually positioned us in the highest place we could possibly be.

> But God, who is rich in mercy, because of His great love with
> which He loved us, even when we were dead in trespasses, made
> us alive together with Christ (by grace you have been saved),
> and raised us up together, and made us sit together in the heav-
> enly places in Christ Jesus.
>
> *Ephesians 2:4-6*

Why did He do this?

...that in the ages to come He might show the exceeding riches of His grace in His kindness toward us in Christ Jesus.

Ephesians 2:7

All our Father wants to do is to be with us and bless us, to work with us and enable us to do what He has called us to do. He wants to be right there and bless us wherever we are. We have to remember that truth at all times, because in this life we are going to suffer from time to time, and when we suffer it will seem like it will never end. At those times, we need to remember that no matter what happens to us, God is for us, not against us. We have to remember that He gave us eternal life so we could live with Him forever when we die, but He gave us resurrection life now to overcome, endure, and persevere when we are confronted with trials and tribulations.

Some people think that the great apostles in the New Testament never got discouraged or depressed, never had to deal with their flesh, but that isn't true. They had to walk this out the same way we do.

Paul's Thorn

And lest I should be exalted above measure by the abundance of the revelations, a thorn in the flesh was given to me, a messenger of Satan to buffet me, lest I be exalted above measure. Concerning this thing I pleaded with the Lord three times that it might depart from me. And He said to me, "My grace is sufficient for you, for My strength is made perfect in weakness."

2 Corinthians 12:7-9

What was Paul complaining about? Many Bible scholars have speculated about what Paul's thorn could have been. One possibility is that everywhere he went, he would preach the Gospel of the grace of God, great revival would come, people would get saved, new churches would be established—and then along came the Judaizers. These were believing Jews who were still living under the Law instead of the grace of God in Christ Jesus. They would tell the new Gentile converts that they had to keep the Law in order to be saved.

Paul loved the people who got saved under his ministry. He cared deeply for them and was very diligent about watching over their souls. These new believers were so happy to be free from the bondage and condemnation of sin. Their hearts overflowed with gratitude that the grace of God saved them when they didn't earn it or deserve it. And they were passionate about getting to know the one true God as their Father. This was the Good News Paul preached and taught.

Then these religious Jews, who believed in Jesus as their Messiah, would come into town and tell the new converts something different: If they didn't learn the Law and keep it, they would not keep their salvation. This is why Paul wrote to the Galatians:

I marvel that you are turning away so soon from Him who called you in the grace of Christ, to a different gospel, which is not another; but there are some who trouble you and want to pervert the gospel of Christ. But even if we, or an angel from heaven, preach any other gospel to you than what we have preached to you, let him be accursed. As we have said before, so now I say again, if anyone preaches any other gospel to you than what you have received, let him be accursed.

Galatians 1:6-9

Can you see why Paul might have been referring to the Judaizers as his "thorn in the flesh"? They stirred up his carnal nature. They made him mad! If there was one thing Paul was passionate about in his ministry, it was the grace of God. No one understood it better, because Paul believed he was the worst of sinners. Before he came to the Lord, he had actually killed Christians!

Resurrection Life Now!

When some of Paul's Jewish brothers did everything they could to wreak havoc in his ministry and put babes in Christ, Paul's children in the Lord, back into the bondage of keeping the Law, he really had to fight his flesh. They certainly acted like a thorn, literally a stake, that the enemy was pounding into his soul, trying to get him to lose his temper and sin.

When Paul realized what the Judaizers were doing, he probably had all kinds of thoughts and pictures go through his mind that were not holy. Thoughts of vengeance and even murder might have been what he struggled with, and it went on for so long that he finally begged God to stop these people from bothering him and his ministry.

If you have ever tried to build a ministry, a business, or a profession for God, you know what Paul was going through. The devil will always send people in to try to sabotage what God wants you to accomplish—and some of these people can be those you know God wanted you to work with! Why would He do that? To keep you humble.

Paul wrote most of the New Testament epistles and had been given the revelation of the mystery of the Church. He was extremely intelligent and very knowledgeable, and the Bible warns that knowledge can puff up a person with pride and arrogance (1 Corinthians 8:1). So God sent this "messenger of Satan," to remind Paul that he didn't know everything and that he had to rely on God's grace alone. He had to forgive and walk humbly in God's wisdom and strength in order to overcome Satan's attack.

The only way Paul could do that was to draw upon the resurrection life of Christ Jesus in him. The Holy Spirit was the only one who could infuse his mind and heart with love and forgiveness. No doubt, again and again he had to exchange his weakness for His strength so he could put to death his flesh and live by the Spirit of life. He had to walk in the very grace he preached!

Resurrection Life Lifts You

Amazing Grace

I want to say a word about the grace of God. So many believers think the grace of God is just for when they get saved. Or they think it is some idea in God's mind that even though they don't deserve to be saved or healed or delivered, He will do that for them because He is a good God. All these things are true, but the grace of God is so much more!

Truly, the grace of God is the resurrection life in you. When trials and troubles come, God's grace lifts you up so that you can persevere, endure, and overcome them. When your business has all but died and you feel like giving up, God's grace will give you the courage to keep going. His resurrection life will make all the dead places in that business come alive again. Grace is not an idea; grace is the power of resurrection life!

I'm not just trying to tie these two things together. In the Greek, the word translated "grace" in 2 Corinthians 12:9 is *charis*, and the gifts of the Spirit in 1 Corinthians 12:4 are called *charisma*,[1] or supernatural manifestations of the grace of God. Grace gifts are another name for the gifts of the Holy Spirit. The same Spirit that raised Jesus from the dead lifts you up through His gifts of grace.

Can you see why the gifts are so important? When you are going through a really rough time, a word of knowledge or wisdom or prophecy can really lift your spirit and give you hope to move forward again. If you are sick, the gifts of healing will certainly lift you up. And if your finances are in a mess, you would really be lifted up by the gifts of faith and miracles!

Beloved, there may be days and times when you, like Paul, will say, "God, this thing is overwhelming me. It is hindering me. I'm really bothered by it all the time. Please, just take it away."

Resurrection Life Now!

God has already answered you in His Word: "My grace is sufficient for you and has lifted you up! You are seated with Me in Heaven. Remember who you are and what I have given you. It doesn't matter what you feel. In My grace and resurrection life you can rise up, go to work, and show and tell everyone that I'm alive and live inside of you. Never mind what's trying to hinder you or pull you down. I am greater! Just trust and rely on My resurrection life inside you, My amazing grace!"

Do you know what I'm talking about? You wake up on Monday morning and can hardly get up or go on. The boss chewed you out last week for an honest mistake. You apologized, made it right, and thought that would be it. But people are talking about you. Your friends at work won't even look at you. Instead of helping you, they have run from you like you have the plague. What do you do?

You must remember how Jesus was resurrected from the dead. Almost everyone He knew and loved had rejected Him, denied Him, and even put Him on the cross. But then Sunday morning came! And the same power that raised Him up dwells in you. Remembering the resurrection life in you, something begins to stir deep inside. Your heart is quickened and begins to pump stronger. The eyes of your understanding are enlightened to new possibilities. Before you know it, you're out of bed, brushing your teeth, and chomping at the bit to get back in the race!

The resurrection life of Jesus Christ has lifted you. The grace of God is sufficient for you. And you can do all things through Christ who strengthens you (Philippians 4:13).

Heavenly Perspective

This is the reality of the Christian life. We have eternal life to live forever with the Lord, but we have resurrection life to lift us above all the difficulties and emotional pains of life that we experience now.

Resurrection Life Lifts You

Christians don't live in a utopia, where everyone treats us the way we want to be treated and we never have any problems in our families, with our friends, or in our work and ministry. We live in a fallen world where people—even our best friends at church—offend us and hurt us.

Some of us have been hurt more than others, but everyone has been hurt. Some have more reason to be angry than others, but we have all been offended. There is someone who experienced ALL emotional pain, and that is Jesus. He took it on the cross, and while He walked this earth with us, He experienced every temptation, trial, and trouble other humans, the world, and the devil could cause Him.

Therefore, in all things He had to be made like His brethren, that He might be a merciful and faithful High Priest in things pertaining to God, to make propitiation for the sins of the people. For in that He Himself has suffered, being tempted, He is able to aid those who are tempted.

Hebrews 2:17-18

Jesus understands what you are going through, but He doesn't stop there. He aids you. He is merciful, and He is faithful. And the greatest thing He has done for you is to give you the gift of the Holy Spirit and deposit His resurrection life in you.

Because you are a child of God now, you have to retrain yourself. Instead of complaining to Him every time something happens that you don't like, begging Him to take it away or remove it, you need to be lifted up and remember that His grace is sufficient. You need to remember that your position in life is not just on this earth but also in Heaven. You are seated with Him in the heavenly realm, and you need to look at your situation from God's perspective. You need to draw upon the grace and resurrection life He gave you because it is not only sufficient but also it will please Him!

Resurrection Life Now!

Honestly, sometimes I don't know how Jesus can sit there and put up with some of the things we say and do, but He does. I mean, we are sitting there, right beside Him, and we act like He is a million miles away and doesn't care. Still, He is merciful and He is faithful. He comes to our aid. And how does He do that? He lifts us up by His resurrection power! He reminds us that we are seated right next to Him and our enemies are under His feet and our feet.

So we need to begin to live from that high place in God, where we sit beside Him in the heavenly realm. We need to stop looking at things from a natural perspective and see our situation from His point of view. Up there, our emotions are not so overpowering and our thinking becomes a lot clearer.

Knowing Him

When you remember that you are lifted up, seated with God in the heavenlies, knowing Him and being in His presence makes every problem you are facing become manageable. He is so big, you can see how really small your problem is. His grace is sufficient. His resurrection life—not the person who just stuck a knife in your back at church—is what overwhelms you. Paul, who dealt with his thorn in the flesh, wrote:

I also count all things loss for the excellence of the knowledge of Christ Jesus my Lord, for whom I have suffered the loss of all things, and count them as rubbish, that I may gain Christ and be found in Him, not having my own righteousness, which is from the law, but that which is through faith in Christ, the righteousness which is from God by faith; that I may know Him and the power of His resurrection, and the fellowship of His sufferings, being conformed to His death, if, by any means, I may attain to the resurrection from the dead.

Philippians 3:8-11

Resurrection Life Lifts You

Paul said, "I have suffered the loss of all things and count it as nothing compared to knowing Christ Jesus." I want you to remember that statement. We cry over the things that we have to lay aside. We weep and mourn and feel so sorry for ourselves. I'm talking about myself! "Oh God, the things I have given up to serve You!" But you know something? It's as nothing. For what I have gained by really putting my life in His hands is far more exciting and fulfilling than I could ever have gotten on my own.

Paul went on to say in verse 10, "...that I may know Him and the power of His resurrection, and the fellowship of His sufferings." What we don't like to face is that to walk in resurrection life, we need to crucify our flesh on the cross—not just once when we get saved but every day. Paul said, "I die daily" (1 Corinthians 15:31), and he obviously wasn't talking about dying spiritually or physically. He was saying that every day he had to put his old carnal nature to death, because if his old, fleshly man was alive, the resurrection life of Christ Jesus inside him would be hindered and even stopped.

Paul wanted to experience Jesus in a greater way. He wanted to understand Him in the power of His resurrection, to experience the power that raised Jesus from the dead. The Greek word for power here is *dunamis*, which we know can mean "moral power and excellence of soul."[2] This is the miraculous power that lifted Jesus up, and it is in you! Your mind, emotions and will can be supernaturally strengthened and empowered to do the right thing.

It is interesting that Paul says he wants to experience the power of Jesus' resurrection, but at the same time he wants to experience the "fellowship of His sufferings." Fellowship is companionship, communion, and joint participation. It is you and your best friend doing something together. Paul wants to know what Jesus' sufferings had to do with him. He wants to really grasp it and understand the whole of it. Why? So he can know Jesus as deeply and intimately as possible.

What Makes You So Different?

In verse 11, Paul goes on to say, "...if, by any means, I may attain to the resurrection from the dead." I like how the Amplified Bible translates it:

That if possible I may attain to the [spiritual and moral] resurrection [that lifts me] out from among the dead [even while in the body].

Philippians 3:11 AMP

We have resurrection life that is spiritual and moral, and we had better understand how to persevere in moral and spiritual resurrection life if we are going to live among "the dead." Who was Paul referring to when he said "the dead"? He was talking about the spiritually dead.

It's likely that not everyone you have contact with in your life is going to get saved. Some of them are going to choose to stay in their trespasses and sins and get as much pleasure out of that immoral life as possible. Furthermore, your brothers and sisters in Christ are not always going to act right toward you or just in general. Some of them might look and act just like the lost and spiritually dead people you rub shoulders with in the world.

Paul had the same experience, and he said he wanted to attain, or get to the point in his life, where he walked in the "spiritual and moral resurrection that lifts me out from among the dead." He wanted to walk in the same resurrection life that raised Jesus from the dead and set Him apart from those who were spiritually dead and separated from the life of God.

Resurrection Life Lifts You

Paul wanted to know and understand experientially the difference that the resurrection life made in Jesus' life so that he could live that way in his life. He wanted to fully walk in the grace that was sufficient for him to overcome, forgive, and move past his thorn in the flesh.

Let me tell you something: Just having the resurrection life on the inside of you doesn't make you different to anyone but God. However, when you walk in resurrection life morally, when you allow that power to manifest in your life in some way, you become different to other people in your life. That's when they see that Jesus is truly alive in you.

First Corinthians 13 tells you that you can move in all the gifts of the Spirit and do great signs and wonders, but if you don't have love, it profits you nothing. You don't get one reward. That is because all those things are obviously supernatural. If a tumor falls off of someone you pray for, people know that's God. They may have more respect for your ability to allow God to work miracles through you, but they won't have any respect for you personally if you do not show integrity of heart.

How are people going to know you're different? When they see how the resurrection life of the Lord Jesus Christ lifts you above hurt and offenses. When you forgive them or someone else for doing damage to your home, for hurting your children, for stealing from you, for taking something that was valuable and precious to you, or for lying and gossiping about you.

Jesus forgave you from the cross, and you have to get your flesh up there with Him every day and forgive those who don't know what they are doing. This is the 1 Corinthians 13 love that will lift you high above the squabbles and conflicts of this world and set you apart from the crowd. This is what Paul meant by understanding and experiencing the power of the resurrection through the fellowship of His sufferings. When you live your life this way, it will bring the lost to your door, saying, "What must I do to be saved?"

Who Gets the Glory?

One of the lies of the devil is that true spiritual maturity means never having a problem, never being hurt, and having it "all together" at all times. The truth is, if we appear really strong and have it all together all the time, that wouldn't give a lot of glory to God. But what if our own strength is not sufficient? We are totally overwhelmed and in something way over our head. There isn't anything we can do to change the situation or make it better. Still, we have faith, trust God, and pray and believe His promises to us. Then wonder of wonders, we get a breakthrough. Our child comes home and goes into a drug rehabilitation program. Our parents decide not to divorce. Our neighbor begins to talk with us again. It's a miracle! Now God gets the glory, and that's the way it should be.

"That's true, Pastor Anne, but what do I get out of this?" You will glory in your weaknesses! You will get to experience what the apostle Paul experienced when he trusted the amazing grace and resurrection life inside him and exchanged his weakness for the strength of God: In your weakness, God's strength is made perfect. He came to your aid. He showed Himself strong on your behalf. Paul said, "I glory in my weaknesses, because when I'm weak, then He's strong."

We cry to God to get us out of things, but He gets more glory and we are a greater witness to the resurrection life of Jesus Christ when we walk through them, trusting Him and praising Him for every inch of ground we take in His name. "Okay Lord, I'm stepping out on the water now. I'm trusting You! I'm walking toward You. Oops! Got to keep my eyes on You. I see that! Help me. Give me understanding. Help me love. Give me Your strength to forgive. Thank You, Lord." And then when you get back in the boat, and Jesus is still there with you, all you can do is praise and worship Him.

Resurrection Life Lifts You

"Nobody knows the trouble I've seen. Nobody knows but Jesus."

These are the words to a famous Negro Spiritual, and they are powerful because they tell us Jesus understands what we are going through. The problem is, many of us are just singing the first line. We forget the second one and decide that we are the only ones suffering for Jesus—or just plain suffering. We get on our high horse of martyrdom and have an all-out pity party, thinking what we are going through is way too hard for any human being, yet God is not removing it from us. I mean, what's the deal?!!!

Whenever I feel like that (and yes, I do from time to time!), I just get out my Bible and read this passage of Scripture:

I've worked much harder, been jailed more often, beaten up more times than I can count, and at death's door time after time. I've been flogged five times with the Jews' thirty-nine lashes, beaten by Roman rods three times, pummeled with rocks once. I've been shipwrecked three times, and immersed in the open sea for a night and a day. In hard traveling year in and year out, I've had to ford rivers, fend off robbers, struggle with friends, struggle with foes. I've been at risk in the city, at risk in the country, endangered by desert sun and sea storm, and betrayed by those I thought were my brothers. I've known drudgery and hard labor, many a long and lonely night without sleep, many a missed meal, blasted by the cold, naked to the weather.

And that's not the half of it, when you throw in the daily pressures and anxieties of all the churches. When someone gets to the end of his rope, I feel the desperation in my bones. When someone is duped into sin, an angry fire burns in my gut.

Resurrection Life Now!

If I have to "brag" about myself, I'll brag about the humiliations that make me like Jesus. The eternal and blessed God and Father of our Master Jesus knows I'm not lying. Remember the time I was in Damascus and the governor of King Aretas posted guards at the city gates to arrest me? I crawled through a window in the wall, was let down in a basket, and had to run for my life.

2 Corinthians 11:23-33 MSG

Jesus had to run for His life several times—we forget that! And Paul was humiliated because he had to run for his life too. He also went through every kind of persecution, physical torture, emotional pain, and even had to endure shipwrecks at sea.

There are several things on this list that I have never had to go through, so reading this always brings me right back where I need to be. I will get through my testings and trials the same way Paul got through his: by allowing the resurrection life of Jesus to lift me up, high above my situation, so I can see and hear what I need to endure, and I can persevere to "get to the other side." His grace is sufficient again and again and again.

Therefore we do not lose heart. Even though our outward man is perishing, yet the inward man is being renewed day by day. For our light affliction, which is but for a moment, is working for us a far more exceeding and eternal weight of glory, while we do not look at the things which are seen, but at the things which are not seen. For the things which are seen are temporary, but the things which are not seen are eternal.

2 Corinthians 4:16-18

Paul refers to all his testings and trials as "light affliction"! Being whipped, stoned, beaten with rods, imprisoned, shipwrecked, bitten by poisonous snakes, and hated by his Jewish people—all this is light affliction? We call it big-time stuff, but he calls it light stuff. And he says it is just for a moment. I'll tell you, one day in that hospital bed, not being able to move, felt like years to me! How could I possibly see those sufferings the way Paul writes about them? I had to be lifted up! Before I was physically out of that bed, I had to be lifted up in my spirit and soul.

I had to look at the things that were not seen instead of the things I was seeing. I had to remember that I was really seated with Jesus in Heaven and this too would pass. I had to remember that I had His resurrection life sustaining me and strengthening me in my inner being. And so, the Holy Spirit healed my physical body. Do you see how being lifted up by the resurrection life inside you can make the difference? Instead of crying, "Nobody knows the trouble I've seen," you will be shouting inside, "Jesus is lifting me!"

Laying Hold

Patience, perseverance, and self-control are the fruit of the Spirit we don't want to face, because they all have to do with challenges, hardships, pain, and suffering. As I said before, just because we are Christians doesn't mean we will never have a problem in life. What makes us different from those who don't know the Lord is not that we never have problems; what makes us different is how we deal with problems. That is a big part of our witness to the world.

Every believer struggles. Paul wrote,

Not that I have already attained, or am already perfected; but I press on, that I may lay hold of that for which Christ Jesus has also laid hold of me.

Philippians 3:12

Resurrection Life Now!

With what did Christ Jesus "lay hold" of Paul? What was Paul talking about? Resurrection life! As soon as we believe Jesus was raised from the dead and confess Him as our Lord, He sends the Holy Spirit to "lay hold" of us. The same Spirit that raised Him from the dead now lives in us.

Paul says that he hasn't been perfected yet, that he hasn't fully grasped the resurrection life that has taken hold of his life. He goes on to say,

> *Brethren, I do not count myself to have apprehended; but one thing I do, forgetting those things which are behind and reaching forward to those things which are ahead, I press toward the goal for the prize of the upward call of God in Christ Jesus.*
>
> *Philippians 3:13-14*

Although he didn't fully understand the resurrection life that was in him, Paul continued to pursue it, to "press toward the goal for the prize." He said, "I'm reaching for it, stretching out toward it. I want to get a hold of resurrection life, to know the Spirit's character and power, to experience the Divine Life and Light that took hold of my life and continues to save me, heal me, deliver me, and give me the strength to endure what is happening right now."

Paul wanted to live for God in the best, most powerful way possible. I do too. I bet you do also, but maybe you say, "I've never been able to really live for God the way I ought to." You need to be filled with the Holy Spirit! He is the resurrection life who lifts you up above any struggle and trial. If you already have been baptized in the Holy Ghost, then begin speaking in tongues and fill yourself up again. Being filled with the Holy Spirit is not a one-time deal! You need to be filled every day, just like you need to die to the flesh every day. In fact, it won't do you much good to die to your flesh if you don't replace that dead flesh with the resurrection life of the Spirit. Then see if you don't have patience, perseverance, and self-control!

Resurrection life will rise up in your spirit and lift up your soul so that you can meet every challenge, face every tragedy, endure every kind of pain, and be a powerful witness for the Lord Jesus Christ. In Him, you can do all things! Resurrection life doesn't bow. He doesn't bend. And He doesn't change. He just does one thing: He gives you the supernatural ability to live for God.

You Are a Member

Before I close this chapter, I want to stress something—you are not alone. "I know Pastor Anne. Jesus is always with me." Yes, that's true, but there's more to that than what you think. You were baptized into the body of Christ. You have a new family, the family of God, and that means you have brothers and sisters and mothers and fathers in the Spirit. You were not born again to sit at home alone, minister alone, or go through testings and trials alone. You were born again to spiritually live and serve God in His family and with His family.

I think you can see that if the saints hadn't prayed for me, and if Robin and the other members of my family hadn't had the faith for me to be healed, I probably would be in Heaven today. Now going to Heaven is not a bad thing unless it isn't your time to go, and it wasn't my time to go. So God used members of our church family to lift me up. Yes, you heard that right. We are to release the resurrection power in us to lift up one another.

I learned this when I first started serving God: No matter what storm I was going through, no matter what tragedy, mountain, or obstacle, if God would talk to me, I could make it through Hell or high water. But I'm not perfect. Like Paul, I haven't attained the full knowledge of the resurrection life inside me. So many times, God uses another member of the body to give me His Word or a word from the Lord that gives me the peace and strength I need to move forward and keep fighting until I get to the place I need to be.

You Can Hear God Through Your Brothers and Sisters!

If I can hear God and I know God is talking to me, I'm lifted up. I'm not dying in this storm! I'm keeping on and going on until the wind calms and the rain becomes a drizzle and the sun begins to shine again. Faith comes by hearing the Word (Romans 10:17), and God speaks His Word to you many times through the very people you see day in and day out. When you realize this, it becomes one of His great miracles in your life.

Beloved, if you are not in a church, get in one! You need to be in a fellowship of believers who will cooperate with the resurrection life of Christ Jesus and lift you up when you are going through fire and flood. Look at me. I'm a pastor, and I needed my church. In fact, I would be dead today if my church had not prayed and contended for my life when I went into total organ failure.

> *Through suffering, our bodies continue to share in the death of Jesus so that the life of Jesus may also be seen in our bodies.*
>
> *Yes, we live under constant danger of death because we serve Jesus, so that the life of Jesus will be evident in our dying bodies.*
>
> *2 Corinthians 4:10-11 NLT*

We are often placed in dire circumstances so that the life of Jesus might be clearly seen in our lives. Yes, we suffer. We don't suffer because God loves to see us suffer. No! He doesn't like to see us suffer any more than we like to see our children suffer. But we don't suffer alone.

Resurrection Life Lifts You

We have each other and the Father, the Son, and the Holy Spirit to lift us up and to keep us going. Then the people in our lives will marvel at how the resurrection life of the Spirit has lifted us up, high above the pain, the suffering, the agony, and the grief; and they will want the Lord and Savior who has brought us through it.

Resurrection Life Now!

Chapter 9

Resurrection Life Authorizes You

You have an enemy, and he wants to kill you.

If he can't kill you, he will do whatever he can to steal from you and destroy your life.

The thief does not come except to steal, and to kill, and to destroy. I have come that they may have life, and that they may have it more abundantly.

John 10:10

One of the reasons God sent Jesus to die for us on the cross was so that we could defeat the devil and all his schemes to entrap us, snare us, put us in bondage to sin, and ruin our lives.

For this purpose the Son of God was manifested, that He might destroy the works of the devil.

1 John 3:8

Jesus defeated Satan. He came to destroy the works of the enemy. He did it to satisfy God and to set us free.

And He said to them, "I saw Satan fall like lightning from heaven. Behold, I give you the authority to trample on serpents and scorpions, and over all the power of the enemy, and nothing shall by any means hurt you."

Luke 10:18-19

Resurrection Life Now!

How much power do we have? We have power over ALL the power of the enemy. Then why are we so afraid? Why do we run? Why do we hide? Why do we shiver and shake? Let someone just mention some of the things the world is reading or seeing in movies, and we turn inside out. We have forgotten the words of Jesus! We have forgotten what He accomplished for us in His death and resurrection: He gave us authority over all the power of the enemy.

Fear or Faith?

Dr. Crandall was filling out the papers indicating the time of death of one of his patients, when he heard the Spirit of God say, "Try one more time." Forty minutes had gone by, and he had used the heart-starting paddles so many times. His mind argued, *The man is dead!* But he heard in his spirit, "Try one more time."

Dr. Crandall stopped writing, turned around, and went back to the dead man. He told the nurse, "We're going to try it one more time." The nurse looked at him incredulously. While she got the paddles, he laid his hands on the corpse and said, "God, if this man isn't saved, let him come back to life and give him one more chance." Then he turned to the nurse and said, "Hit him again." She hit him with the paddles, and they heard a perfect heart beat.

That was resurrection life authorizing my brother, a great doctor of medicine, to raise a man from the dead. Why? Satan had done his worst. He had killed a man who did not know Jesus as his Lord and Savior. He had killed him and sent him to Hell. But Dr. Crandall knew his authority in Christ Jesus, and I'm sure that man thanked him for using it!

Resurrection Life Authorizes You

Inasmuch then as the children have partaken of flesh and blood, He Himself likewise shared in the same, that through death He might destroy him who had the power of death, that is, the devil, and release those who through fear of death were all their lifetime subject to bondage.

Hebrews 2:14-15

Beloved, because Jesus was resurrected and we believed it and received Him as our Lord, we never have to fear death or live in the bondage of fear again! The same Spirit that raised Jesus lives in us and authorizes us to prevent and undo any works of the devil and his demons. However, in order to do that, we have to have faith. Faith releases the resurrection life in us to destroy the works of the enemy. Fear, on the other hand, opens the door for the enemy to come in and do his worst.

You ask, "How can I have faith when something is scaring me to death?" You are going to have a lot more faith and a lot less fear when you meditate on God's Word. I have said this before and will say it again and again: Romans 10:17 says that faith comes by hearing the Word of God. So the more you read, study, and meditate in God's Word, the more faith you are going to have. You can also build your faith by praying in your prayer language (Jude 1:20).

Unfortunately, the devil knows this also. Do you ever notice how many interruptions happen when you sit down to read the Bible or pray? Suddenly you remember all the things you forgot to do. Now if God wants to spend some quality time with you, who do you think is giving you that to-do list?

I was starting to study one morning and remembered something I had to do. I stopped and I went to do it, thinking, *Well, I'll just praise and sing to the Lord for awhile.* Then I came back to study and something else came to mind. I said, "Oh, I gotta go do this." Halfway there I thought, *This is ridiculous. Not doing that anymore.* I recognized that the enemy was trying to keep me from getting into the Word of God and hearing from the Holy Spirit. If I wanted to really do everything God had called me to do in the power of His resurrection, I needed to get my act together and build my faith.

Another thing you have to understand is that faith and fear are spiritual attitudes, not emotions. You can be feeling all kinds of terrible emotions and still have faith to move mountains. Just like you were saved by grace through faith, the resurrection life in you is released by grace through faith. It doesn't matter how you feel, choose to have faith instead of fear and you will move that mountain out of your life!

Jesus said,

"Have faith in God. For assuredly, I say to you, whoever says to this mountain, 'Be removed and be cast into the sea,' and does not doubt in his heart, but believes that those things he says will be done, he will have whatever he says. Therefore I say to you, whatever things you ask when you pray, believe that you receive them, and you will have them."

Mark 11:22-24

Do you realize that your spirit is full of faith because that is where the Spirit of faith lives? Your spirit and your heart are the same thing. If you do not doubt in your spirit that Jesus was raised from the dead, then you can choose not to doubt in your heart and believe that what you are praying will come to pass—regardless of how you feel emotionally. Just make sure what you are believing and praying is the will of God! When you pray according to His will and Word, the Holy Spirit and the angels of the Lord go forth to answer. Hebrews 1:14 says the angels are also under your authority. They are standing by, waiting to hear your instructions:

Are they not all ministering spirits sent forth to minister for those who will inherit salvation?

Who is inheriting salvation? Those who believe Jesus was raised from the dead and call Him their Lord. You and I have an inheritance of salvation—being continuously saved by the resurrection life of Christ Jesus.

Your Inheritance

In Him also we have obtained an inheritance....

In Him you also trusted, after you heard the word of truth, the gospel of your salvation; in whom also, having believed, you were sealed with the Holy Spirit of promise, who is the guarantee of our inheritance until the redemption of the purchased posses-sion, to the praise of His glory.

Ephesians 1:11, 13-14

Your inheritance is awesome. You are not only going to Heaven to live with God forever in perfect health and well-being, with every-thing you could possibly ask or think or imagine, but also you have the privilege of bringing Heaven to earth right now. How do you do that? Through the resurrection life that is in you by the Holy Spirit. He is the guarantee of your inheritance.

You are "in Him." That means you've got a divine spark on the inside of you. You've got something supernatural working in you and upon you. And it is through the power of the Holy Spirit that you walk in authority over the enemy today. You can look forward to the day when your body will be redeemed and your soul fully transformed, but until then you have the guarantee living inside you. He gives you all spiritual blessings.

> *Blessed be the God and Father of our Lord Jesus Christ, who has blessed us with every spiritual blessing in the heavenly places in Christ.*
>
> *Ephesians 1:3*

> *But God, ... raised us up together, and made us sit together in the heavenly places in Christ Jesus.*
>
> *Ephesians 2:4, 6*

You walk on this Earth in the natural, but you live in a higher realm in the Spirit. You sit in heavenly places with Christ Jesus. You live above the evil of this world and the enemy who is behind it. Satan is called "the prince of the power of the air" in Ephesians 2:2. He and his demons move around in the atmosphere where you breathe air. That means that spiritually you sit with Jesus far above him. You can't defeat the devil in your natural abilities, but in the Spirit all evil is under your authority in Christ Jesus.

That's why the stock market has nothing to do with your prosperity. Banks don't supply your needs. You know the God who can bring water out of a rock! There is nothing the enemy can pull that the Spirit of God does not have the upper hand.

> *When the enemy comes in like a flood,*
>
> *The Spirit of the LORD will lift up a standard against him.*
>
> *Isaiah 59:19*

What is the standard the Spirit of the Lord lifts up every time the enemy attacks a child of God? Jesus is alive! He has risen! And the same Spirit that raised Him from the dead dwells in you. The flag of victory you carry in your heart is the flag of resurrection life in Christ Jesus. His resurrection gives you full authority over the enemy.

What Reigns in Your Life?

How does the enemy most often attack you? You need to know this if you are going to successfully defeat him in your life. He attacks you in your mind. We saw this in Chapter 6, discussing how we need to renew our minds with the Word of God to transform our souls. But let's look at this from a different angle.

If you have full authority over the devil, then somehow he has to get you to give him permission to do something in you, through you, or because of you. He does this through deception and lies, which you can defeat by simply going to the Word and the Spirit of God and taking every thought captive, making your life obedient to Jesus Christ (2 Corinthians 10:3-5). But I'll tell you what he uses more than anything else: your own lust.

Where do wars and fights come from among you? Do they not come from your desires for pleasure that war in your members? You lust and do not have.

James 4:1-2

All sin comes from self-centered selfishness, and if the devil can get you to think you ought to have something you don't have, something you really want, then he's got you under his control. There are all kinds of sins, but they fall into one of these three categories:

Do not love the world or the things in the world. If anyone loves the world, the love of the Father is not in him. For all that is in the world—the lust of the flesh, the lust of the eyes, and the pride of life—is not of the Father but is of the world.

1 John 2:15-16

- the lust of the eyes – money and worldly riches

- the lust of the flesh – physical gratification of any kind

- the pride of life – power and supremacy over others

These are Satan's three strategies to get you distracted and eventually completely off-track from serving God. So you have to decide every morning to die to your flesh and live by the Spirit, and sometimes you have to make that decision again and again all day long! You have to decide that the resurrection life on the inside of you will reign in your heart and mind and body and soul. You must say, "I no longer serve sin; I serve the living Lord Jesus. I have His resurrection life in me to do it."

Now if we died with Christ, we believe that we shall also live with Him, ... He died to sin once for all; but the life that He lives, He lives to God. Likewise you also, reckon yourselves to be dead indeed to sin, but alive to God in Christ Jesus our Lord.

Therefore do not let sin reign in your mortal body, that you should obey it in its lusts. And do not present your members as instruments of unrighteousness to sin, but present yourselves to God as being alive from the dead, and your members as instruments of righteousness to God. For sin shall not have dominion over you, for you are not under law but under grace.

Romans 6:8, 10-14

Beloved, if we reckoned ourselves dead unto sin, we wouldn't be running after it so much. To reckon means to declare that something is a fact, and we are to declare that we are dead to sin and alive to God. Therefore, we no longer obey the lusts of our flesh; we obey the Spirit and the Word—that's how grace works. It's how resurrection life works. We aren't going around keeping this law and that law; we are alive to

God in Christ Jesus our Lord and walk with Him, doing His will and Word, by the power of His Spirit.

We are to present ourselves to God as being dead to sin and alive to Him. And when sin knocks on our door, or when temptation corners us, James gives us the way out:

> *Therefore submit to God. Resist the devil and he will flee from you. Draw near to God and He will draw near to you.*
>
> *James 4:7-8*

Here's the formula to defeat the devil when he tries to get you to sin:

1. Submit your weakness to God immediately. Exchange your weakness for His strength. Get His perspective of your situation. In doing this, you resist the devil's attempts to get you to sin and put you in bondage.

2. The devil will flee because you have resisted him. You have told him no.

3. Draw near to God even more after the devil flees, because it is when you get the victory that you think you can do it on your own. You can't ever do it on your own! You always need to draw near to God and have His resurrection life fill you with the joy and wisdom you need to live free from sin.

This is the way you let the Spirit, not the flesh, reign in your life, and if the Spirit is reigning, the devil has no way into your family, your ministry, or your business. He can't find any sin to hook you and captivate you and draw you away from God and His will. If Satan comes anywhere near you, he'll only find himself face to face with the one person he doesn't want to see: the King of kings and Lord of lords who defeated him and humiliated him! Do you see that you can't even take credit for defeating the enemy?

Resurrection Life Now!

Submit yourself to God. Resist the devil. He will flee. And draw nearer to God than ever before. This will keep you humble and out of the devil's influence so that sin will not reign in your life; Jesus will.

You Are Far Above All

...the eyes of your understanding being enlightened; that you may know what is the hope of His calling, what are the riches of the glory of His inheritance in the saints, and what is the exceeding greatness of His power toward us who believe, according to the working of His mighty power which He worked in Christ when He raised Him from the dead and seated Him at His right hand in the heavenly places, far above all principality and power and might and dominion, and every name that is named, not only in this age but also in that which is to come.

And He put all things under His feet, and gave Him to be head over all things to the church, which is His body, the fullness of Him who fills all in all.

Ephesians 1:18-23

Unbelievers are clueless to what is going on in the spirit realm, but you have been seated with Jesus in heavenly places and are enlightened. You can know "His mighty power which He worked in Christ when He raised Him from the dead and seated Him at His right hand in the heavenly places." How can you see and know these things? The same Spirit that raised Jesus lives in you. You are seated with Him. Far above all principality. AND power and might and dominion. AND every name that is named now and forever. I love that!

"Principality" means "the princes or chiefs among angels; among demons."[1]

Resurrection Life Authorizes You

"Power" indicates "ability ... authority, jurisdiction, liberty, power, right, strength."[2]

"Might" speaks of "persons in authority, the mighty, the powerful ones."[3]

"Dominion" means "lord, mighty one.... civil power, authority or magistracy."[4]

These words let us know that angels, demons, Satan himself, and every person in a position of strength, influence, or authority, is subject to the Lord Jesus Christ. But that is not all! Ephesians 1:21 goes on to say that every name that is named, both today and tomorrow, is under His feet. I think that just about covers everything!

Ephesians 1:22 confirms that everything is under Jesus' feet. In the Orient, the conquering king put his foot on his foe, the vanquished, to demonstrate to the multitudes that he now ruled him and his kingdom. God has put Jesus' foot on everything and everyone that exists for all time. Jesus is the Supreme Ruler over all things forever.

And He Has Given Us His Authority!

Since we are in Jesus and He is in us, all these things are under our feet as well. God says Jesus is our head. He will tell us when and where and over whom we are to take authority. We are to use the authority He has given us according to His instructions, as His Word and will command us. We are to live by the Spirit, the resurrection life in us, not our flesh or our natural thinking. Sometimes there is strategic timing involved, and when we are dealing with a cunning enemy like Satan, we want to be certain we are acting according to the will of God. Then we can take authority with full confidence.

Having disarmed principalities and powers, He made a public spectacle of them, triumphing over them in it.

Colossians 2:15

Resurrection Life Now!

When the apostle Paul wrote this, I'm sure he was thinking about how Caesar treated the royalty of the nations he conquered. He would strip them of all their royal garments and march them through the public streets, so they looked like common peasants. Caesar would sit high on a moving platform or a large warhorse, following behind them. This was the way he made it known to all the people that the enemy king and queen and all their descendants and subjects were now under him.

As Paul was writing this, I believe he saw into the spirit realm and had a vision of how Jesus stripped Satan and all his demons of all their power, then paraded them through the public streets in complete triumph. We need to get this picture firmly planted in our minds and hearts. Jesus has stripped the enemy of all authority and is far above them.

He Cannot Swallow You

Be sober, be vigilant; because your adversary the devil walks about like a roaring lion, seeking whom he may devour. Resist him, steadfast in the faith.

1 Peter 5:8-9

Living the Christian life is not sitting back, taking a nap. The resurrection life in you will not automatically handle every attack of the enemy. No, you must do war against the devil. You must be sober and vigilant, never letting down your guard. You don't have to be afraid and uptight, but you do need to stay spiritually in tune with the Holy Spirit. Why? The Word tells us the devil is like a roaring lion, and he will try to fake you out with skirmishes. If he can scare you so badly that you forget who you are and what you have in Christ Jesus, then he can devour you.

Resurrection Life Authorizes You

On the other hand, if you are communing with the Holy Spirit and sense something or He warns you, you can be ready for the enemy. You can resist him, remain steadfast in your faith, and the resurrection life of Christ Jesus will hit him right in the face. He will turn tail and run for the hills because there is no way he can swallow Jesus!

Remember when the magicians of Pharaoh's court challenged Moses to a supernatural duel in Exodus 7:8-12? Aaron threw down his rod and it turned into a serpent. The magicians did the same thing and their rods became serpents too. However, the serpent of Aaron proceeded to swallow all the others' serpents.

Just keep your spiritual eyes and ears open, keep the faith, and the only swallowing that will happen is when the resurrection life in you swallows the enemy!

You Come in THE Name

And being found in appearance as a man, He humbled Himself and became obedient to the point of death, even the death of the cross. Therefore God also has highly exalted Him and given Him the name which is above every name, that at the name of Jesus every knee should bow, of those in heaven, and of those on earth, and of those under the earth, and that every tongue should confess that Jesus Christ is Lord, to the glory of God the Father.

Philippians 2:8-11

God gave Jesus a name that is above every name. "Every name" means every thing and every being in Heaven, on earth, and in Hell. What is the name God has given His Son, the name that is far above any name that can be uttered or mentioned in this world? Lord Jesus Christ.

Resurrection Life Now!

Jesus of Nazareth could be just another guy who lived in Nazareth, a carpenter's son. There were lots of men named Jesus in that time among the Jews. And it's not that different today in some communities. Every Hispanic community has a few men named Jesus (pronounced hay-sus). The name Jesus was pretty common back then, and it still is today.

Jesus Christ would set Him apart from your average Jesus. Christ designates Him as the Anointed One, the Messiah, who had supernatural abilities and great wisdom. But when you put Lord on the front of Jesus Christ, you have just said that He is the King of the Universe, the Ancient of Days, the Alpha and Omega, the One who is and was and always will be. Frankly, I've never known anyone named Lord Jesus Christ except Him.

There is only one Messiah, Savior, and Lord, and that is the Lord Jesus Christ. What will every tongue confess? That Jesus Christ is Lord. When you come in His name, you come in the full authority and are backed up by the sovereign power of Almighty God himself. Are you getting this?!!!

When you get between a rock and a hard place, just declare the Word and will of the Lord Jesus Christ. Just mention the name of Jesus, and everything within the sound of your voice must bow. What makes them bow? The resurrection life of the Holy Spirit that is working right now.

Remember when Peter and John healed the lame man at the Gate Beautiful? The people came rushing out to see what had happened and Peter addressed them:

> *"Men of Israel, why do you marvel at this? Or why look so intently at us, as though by our own power or godliness we had*

made this man walk? The God of Abraham, Isaac, and Jacob, the God of our fathers, glorified His Servant Jesus,.... And His name, through faith in His name, has made this man strong, whom you see and know."

Acts 3:12-13, 16

I got to thinking that it's hard to have faith in a name. Then I thought that maybe it isn't either. If I pick up a brand new can of cold soda and it has the name Coca-Cola on it, I've got confidence it's going to taste like a Coke because it has the name of Coke. When I buy detergent, I don't buy just any detergent. I buy the one I know works the best for me. How do I know it's the best for me? I know by the name on the box.

When you use the name of the Lord Jesus Christ, you know what you're getting—and so does the devil! He hates that name and doesn't want you to use it because when you do, he has to do whatever you tell him to do. He has to bow. He has to leave. He has to stop. He has to be quiet. He has to follow your instructions to the letter!

When you call upon that name that's above every name, demons tremble. And when you preach the Lord Jesus Christ is alive and well, Satan grinds his teeth, just like he did when Peter preached:

Now as they spoke to the people, the priests, the captain of the temple, and the Sadducees came upon them, being greatly disturbed that they taught the people and preached in Jesus the resurrection from the dead. And they laid hands on them, and put them in custody until the next day, for it was already evening. However, many of those who heard the word believed; and the number of the men came to be about five thousand.

Acts 4:1-4

Resurrection Life Now!

What were the priests, the captain of the Temple, and the Sadducees upset about? They were furious that Peter and the other disciples were teaching the people that Jesus had risen from the dead. Of course, these religious people were under Satan's influence, so they went into a rage at just the mention of the name of Jesus. You see, Satan knows the power in the name that is above every other name. Unfortunately, he might believe it more than we do. We need to grasp the authority we have in Jesus' name!

A story my husband John used to tell demonstrates the authority we have in Jesus' name. He was in a drug rehabilitation center in New York, and there was a tremendous blizzard. The roads were iced over, and the snowstorm had left huge, tall drifts. There was no way they could get food from New York City because all the roads were closed. They had run out of food, and so they prayed and worshipped God all night.

The next morning, someone opened the front door of the camp facility, and there was a buck lying on the porch. Not on the steps. Not in the front yard. After being shot, it had made it all the way up the steps to the porch and then dropped dead. John said they were all praising the Lord and practically turning back flips over this miraculous answer to prayer.

This illustrates our authority over every name that is named, even a deer! No matter what the devil throws at you, you can pray in the authority of the name of the Lord Jesus Christ and come through.

Jesus Is Greater

I think this is the hour when the Church will get hold of our authority in Christ Jesus. He has terrified us, squashed us, sat on us, kicked us, bound us, tied us up, and even killed us. Now it's time to draw on the resurrection life inside us and shout, "Enough!"

Resurrection Life Authorizes You

You are of God, little children, and have overcome them, because He who is in you is greater than he who is in the world.

1 John 4:4

I want you to let this truth go deep inside you: The resurrection life that authorizes you to defeat the enemy will see that nothing can kill you, stop you, or keep you from fulfilling the plan of God for your life. All you have to do is do what you are authorized to do: Defeat and overcome the enemy by the blood of the Lamb and the word of your testimony (Revelation 12:11). Keep your spiritual eyes and ears open. Stay in faith. Remember that you sit in the heavenlies and come in the name of the Lord Jesus Christ, declaring the will and Word of God. The Spirit that raised Jesus from the dead will do the rest.

Resurrection Life Now!

Chapter 10

Resurrection Life Perfects You Now

What are the keys to being perfected in Jesus Christ? The obvious and well-taught answers are to read, study, and meditate in God's Word. Pray without ceasing, in the Spirit and in your own language. Fellowship with the saints and be a functioning, vital member of your local church. Minister in some capacity because we are all ministers of reconciliation. These are all important, but I believe we might be making it too complicated.

My husband John loved to tell this testimony of something God did in his life that changed him dramatically. It happened before we were married. He was staying at Brother Minor's house, and it was during the night. John was sleeping on a cot. He didn't know if he was dreaming or if he was awake, but he smelled something terrible. When he opened his eyes, he saw bars in front of him and he realized he was in a prison cell. It was filled with the most horrible stench.

He felt like somebody else was on the cot with him, so he turned to see who it was. What he saw filled him with revulsion. He saw a decomposed corpse with a long beard and long hair, and he was filthy. Then God spoke to him something that changed him forever.

John began to holler and cry out to God, repenting, praying in tongues, and praying in English. Brother and Sister Minor could hear him yelling, but they knew he was having a powerful experience with God, so they did not go to him. Later John told them what had happened. God had said to him:

"Why are you still in bed with your old man?"

One of the hardest things for a pastor to watch is when people get saved, the Lord begins to turn their lives around, and for some reason they sink back into their old way of living. Some still come to church from time to time, but it's like they just keep going back to dabbling in the life of what the Bible calls their "old man." Now if you're a woman, don't get offended. The Bible calls it the old man because in the days it was written, people understood that "man" meant human beings. So just to keep it simple, I'm going to use the biblical term "old man."

Put off, concerning your former conduct, the old man which grows corrupt according to the deceitful lusts, and be renewed in the spirit of your mind, and that you put on the new man which was created according to God, in true righteousness and holiness.

Ephesians 4:22-24

This is the way I see it. If you're really born from above and you're for real, you ought to be running for God so hard and fast that you stir up such dust nobody can even see who it is who is running. God gets all the glory! But I see a lot of believers hanging on to their old man, the person they thought they were or used to want to be, and all the things they wanted to do and did do before they got saved. These could be good things, like becoming an astronaut, or bad things, like doing drugs, but they are holding onto them when God has something greater for them.

Resurrection Life Perfects You Now

I hear Christians say things like, "I need to do this. I just deserve this. I'm tired and I better take a break, kick back, and forget I'm a Christian for awhile. I'm going to enjoy the things of the world a little bit."

I want to shake them and say, "Yes, God wants you to rest and have fun and be refreshed—with Him! That's the only place you are going to get renewed and refired. It will never happen by going back and embracing the thoughts, habits, desires, and behavior of your old man. That's only going to bring you frustration, confusion, and severe shame and pain."

The world laughs at living a holy life for God, and they mock Christians who are living like Jesus. But the Bible says that the last laugh will go to the Father.

The wicked plots against the just, and gnashes at him with his teeth. The Lord laughs at him, for He sees that his day is coming.

Psalm 37:12-13

One day those who have rejected the Lord and made fun of His servants will stand before Him and give an account of their lives. It won't be fun, exciting, or pleasant in any way!

Then I saw a great white throne and Him who sat on it.... And I saw the dead, small and great, standing before God, and books were opened. And another book was opened, which is the Book of Life. And the dead were judged according to their works, by the things which were written in the books. And anyone not found written in the Book of Life was cast into the lake of fire.

Revelation 20:11-12, 15

When we gave our lives to Jesus Christ, that person who loved to sin, acted like the world, and danced to the devil's tune was crucified with Christ. And yet, we go back to being like that old man. This is what my husband John had to face that terrible night at Brother Minor's house. And I have to tell you, from that night on he was changed. He never wanted to have anything to do with the stench of sin and death of his old man again. He spent the rest of his life putting on the new man God had made him to be in Christ Jesus.

Not a lot of churches are talking about this today, but as believers, we will also stand before Jesus and give an account of our lives. For us, this day will be marked by God's mercy and grace toward us. It is when we will be rewarded for all we have done in the name of the Lord Jesus Christ, and everything we did not do for Him will be burned up and gone forever, never to condemn us or cause us shame again.

> For no other foundation can anyone lay than that which is laid, which is Jesus Christ. Now if anyone builds on this foundation with gold, silver, precious stones, wood, hay, straw, each one's work will become clear; for the Day will declare it, because it will be revealed by fire; and the fire will test each one's work, of what sort it is. If anyone's work which he has built on it endures, he will receive a reward. If anyone's work is burned, he will suffer loss; but he himself will be saved, yet so as through fire.
>
> *1 Corinthians 3:11-15*

Everything we have done will be hit by the purifying fire of the Holy Spirit. What we have done for God will become gold, silver, and precious stones that will remain for eternity. What we did not do for Him will become wood, hay, or straw; and mercifully, those dead works will burn up and be forgotten.

As for me, when the fire hits I want a gigantic mountain of gold, silver, and precious stones! If possible, I don't even want a puff of smoke from anything else. And really, the only believers who should be "saved, yet so as through fire," are those who got saved on their deathbed. Those of us who have lived some years in the Lord hopefully have lived for Him and not ourselves.

"My goodness, Pastor Anne! You sure have gotten serious." You bet I have! The most important issue in anyone's life is whether or not they give their lives to the Lord Jesus Christ, and after that the most important issue is whether or not they live for the Lord Jesus Christ. Give it and then live it! If they keep going back to embrace that stinky, corrupt, perverse old man, they are going to have a bonfire on that day, and in the meantime they will live far below the abundant life Jesus died to give them.

"But Pastor Anne, I've tried and tried and I just keep falling. I feel like the biggest disappointment to the Lord." Beloved, that's why I'm writing this book. It's for you. I want you to realize that you've got the same Spirit that raised Jesus from the dead in you! Resurrection life is not only about Easter and the end times. Resurrection life is in you, right now, to perfect you, to grow you and mature you. The resurrection power of the Holy Spirit wants to help you be all God created you to be right now!

You cannot do this in your own strength. You can only find your life by losing it in Him. When you give Him full access to every area of your life, then you will live as He lives. That is the miracle of resurrection life now, and it is how you put off the old man and put on the new!

Let Your Treasure Shine

For it is the God who commanded light to shine out of darkness, who has shone in our hearts to give the light of the knowledge of the glory of God in the face of Jesus Christ.

Resurrection Life Now!

But we have this treasure in earthen vessels, that the excellence of the power may be of God and not of us.

1 Corinthians 4:6-7

This treasure—the light that dispels darkness and the life that brings dead things to life—is in you and me! The glory and shining presence of God, the same Spirit that raised Jesus from the dead, lives in our earthen vessel.

The Church has never fully lived like it.

We go around talking about how depressed we are. "Oh, I'm having a bad day. I'm really down. It seems like I never have enough money. Every time I think my kids are going to be all right, one of them does something really stupid. My boss doesn't appreciate all the extra things I do. My spouse seems to have forgotten I'm alive. I just don't know how much longer I can take this." Many of us are on medication to get us through the day or to sleep at night. Some of us are so wrapped up in our old man that we couldn't see who we are in Christ Jesus if lightning struck us!

I want to shake us all and cry, "Wake up! This is it! This is the best thing that has ever come down the pike for us!"

You ask, "What's got into you, Pastor?"

The resurrection life of God is in me, and it's in you too!

I'm praying and believing for the Church to manifest the amazing treasure inside her. I'm seeing a Bride of Christ whose face is glowing with the light of God inside her and bold as a lion because of the fire in her belly. And that can start with you and me right now.

Resurrection Life Perfects You Now

Hear It!

I believe you and I are in a season where we are going to know walking in the Spirit like we've never known it before. What I mean by that is, we have spiritual senses just like we have natural senses. In the natural we have five senses: seeing, hearing, smelling, tasting, and touching. Our spirit also has these senses and more. We have a sense of discernment, of knowing what is really happening in a natural situation because we know what is going on in the spirit realm.

We do not look at the things which are seen, but at the things which are not seen. For the things which are seen are temporary, but the things which are not seen are eternal.

2 Corinthians 4:18

No wonder the world thinks truly spiritual believers are crazy! They cannot possibly understand us because we are spiritual and they are still just natural human beings. We are looking at things that are not seen in the natural realm. We are experiencing eternal things through our spiritual senses.

What is really sad is believers who have spiritual senses and don't use them. They are too caught up with their natural senses and the world. My prayer is that with a revelation of the resurrection life of God on the inside of them, the Church will have ears to hear what the Spirit is telling the churches.

I believe there is a wisdom and understanding of the spiritual dimension that you and I are coming into in this season. I believe it's a time of spiritual growth and spiritual maturity. We are going to develop the spiritual sense of hearing. We are going to have ears to hear what the Spirit of God is saying, whispering, and nudging us to say and do.

Resurrection Life Now!

We cannot stay as we are. We can't stay immature, acting like spiritual babes (or the old man) after being saved for twenty years. We just can't stay there and fulfill God's plan for His Church. Now there are a lot of believers who want to stay there. They only want to know enough to miss Hell and make Heaven. That's all. Their idea of the cross is that they are forgiven no matter what they do or how they live their lives. But the cross is about a totally, radically changed life! A resurrection life now!

I'll tell you, we are in for the greatest ride of our life if we can just hear and obey what the Holy Spirit is speaking to us in this hour. Don't be surprised. God will speak scriptures to you in the daytime and you'll say, "Oh, I never thought about it that way before." You're going to look in your Bible and find it and write it down. Start writing down what God tells you. And then live it! We all want that new revelation, but after the thrill is gone, we never actually live it out. Let's change that! Let's hear and then obey.

See It

I've been really praying, "Oh God, I want to see. I want to see in the Spirit." Remember Elisha's servant, who got up one morning, went out to fetch water, and saw that the entire city was surrounded by the great Syrian army. He ran back in the house to tell Elisha, who said,

> *"Do not fear, for those who are with us are more than those who are with them." And Elisha prayed, and said, "LORD, I pray, open his eyes that he may see." Then the LORD opened the eyes of the young man, and he saw. And behold, the mountain was full of horses and chariots of fire all around Elisha.*
>
> *2 Kings 6:16-17*

Resurrection Life Perfects You Now

I'm praying what Elisha prayed both for myself and for the body of Christ. It's time we opened our spiritual eyes and allowed God to show us what's really going on in our world! But He's not going to do that if we won't do what He says. The mark of maturity is not a supernatural gift or ability alone, but also the willingness and obedience to act according to God's will.

Remember when Elijah asked Elisha what he wanted above all else, before Elijah left him and went to Heaven? Elisha said that he wanted a double portion of Elijah's Spirit, whom we know was the Holy Spirit. This is what Elijah said to him: "You have asked a hard thing" (2 Kings 2:10). This was not a hard thing for Elijah to grant nor a hard thing for God to do. It was hard because Elijah knew the personal cost of walking in God's power.

Those who are hungry for the supernatural power of God also must be hungry to grow in the character of God. That is the perfection that we can all achieve if we walk in resurrection life now. We can be strong and yet humble, just like Elisha proved to be. He did twice the miracles Elijah had done, but his life was marked by more stability and integrity of soul as well.

God's going to let us see some things that are going to thrill us beyond expression. We're moving forward in the purpose and the plan of God for this world, not just for us as individuals but also for this world. And part of God's purpose and plan, and really the centerpiece of it, is to present to His Son a Bride that is without spot or wrinkle. He's going to have a mature people.

We have to at least have a remnant of mature believers because in these last days we are going to hear and see some things in the Church as well as in the world that will require maturity. The other day I read something a minister said that amused me. He said, "We're living in a time when the two witnesses are going to be seen." (See Revelation 11:1-13.) That may be true, but then he went on to say, "In fact, I saw two of them down in Florida." That's when I rolled my eyes. What he was saying was preposterous. His statement does not line up with the Word of God.

There also have been a lot of believers deciding their gifts and callings. This is another thing God is correcting. You can't take on the office of pastor any more than you can say you are a doctor without going to medical school or having any knowledge of medicine at all. God must call you and give you the gifts to fulfill what He has called you to do. Then the resurrection life on the inside of you can be fully activated and functional. But you have to see it first! Ask God to open your eyes and show you who you are in Him. He may not give you the whole picture, but He will give you enough to take that first step of faith.

God is moving by His Spirit, and He's telling us to grow up in both our spiritual abilities and the character of Christ. It's time to quit letting ourselves get caught up in animosity, anger, bitterness, and resentment. A few years back God spoke to me, "There are three things I'm going to deal with in the Church severely and swiftly. The Church can no longer afford the luxury of these sins." In other words, we can no longer afford the cost we pay (souls lost and a divided Church) by committing these sins. He said, "Number one, I'm going to deal with denominational walls. Number two, I'm going to deal with prejudice against women. And number three, I'm going to deal with racial prejudice in the Church."

Now I'm not going to go into these things in depth, but I want to make the point that no matter what sin you are struggling against, you can't defeat it in your own strength. You have got to have and be filled with the supernatural power of the Spirit. You have to draw on

Resurrection Life Perfects You Now

God's resurrection life to live like Jesus in this world. Resurrection life perfects you now!

Likewise, we as the Church cannot win the world in our own strength. We need to live from that treasure inside us, walking in newness of life. We need to leave that old man in the grave where he belongs, live by our spiritual senses, and obey the Word and the Spirit.

A Challenge

Today I'm running for God with everything in me, and I'm expecting to see things I've never seen and hear things I've never heard. I'm expecting the spirit of revelation to explode in my life and in the life of the Church. I'm expecting miracles and signs and wonders to follow me wherever I go, and I'm doing everything I know to do to put off that old man and grow up into the new creation I am in Christ Jesus. I'm expecting all this for you too.

You are alive to God through Christ Jesus our Lord. That means you are strong, active, powerful, and full of His vigor. Your enemy has been defeated, you have God's supernatural ability to resist temptation and eradicate sin from your life. You are a spiritual child of the Almighty God, and that means you live by the Spirit and not the flesh.

You have everything going for you because the same Spirit that raised Jesus from the dead lives in you.

- God's gift of resurrection life was established before the foundation of the world for you and is now before you, calling you and equipping you to fulfill your divine purpose.
- God's gift of resurrection life saved you and continues to save you every moment of every day.
- God's gift of resurrection life restored your relationship with God so you can know Him intimately.

Resurrection Life Now!

- God's gift of resurrection life endues you with power from on high to be an effective witness for the Lord Jesus Christ.

- God's gift of resurrection life empowers you with supernatural abilities.

- God's gift of resurrection life enlightens your mind and heart with truth that sets you free.

- God's gift of resurrection life quickens and makes healthy and whole your physical body.

- God's gift of resurrection life lifts you up to sit with Jesus, giving you His perspective and infusing you with His strength to endure.

- God's gift of resurrection life authorizes you to defeat the enemy.

- God's gift of resurrection life perfects you now.

If this book rocks the boat, great! Not only do I want to rock the boat, I want us to get out of the boat. I want us to walk on water. And I believe we can.

I'll tell you what this comes down to for you and for me. It's like God dropped a $100,000 car in our driveway. It is the most powerful piece of machinery on the road. Nothing else can touch it for speed, for reliability, for comfort, and to get us where we need to go—and all we do is look at it.

Some of us walk around it. Others touch it here and there. Most of us are in awe of it. But we never get into this amazing gift of God to let Him show us what He can do.

I want to get in and go. What about you?

Endnotes

1 – Resurrection Life Before You

[1]StudyLight.org, definition of Greek word translated "press". http://www.studylight.org/isb/view.cgi? number=1377.

[2]James Strong, *Exhaustive Concordance of the Bible*, "Greek Dictionary of the New Testament" (Nashville, TN: Thomas Nelson Publishers, 1984), #2821.

3 – Resurrection Life Restores You

[1]James Strong, *Exhaustive Concordance of the Bible*, "Hebrew and Chaldee Dictionary" (Nashville, TN: Thomas Nelson Publishers, 1984), #4191.

[2]James Strong, *Exhaustive Concordance of the Bible*, "Greek Dictionary of the New Testament," #5048.

4 – Resurrection Life Endues You

[1]Ibid., #907.

[2]Spiros Zodhiates, *The Complete Word Study Dictionary: New Testament* (Chattanooga, TN: AMG Publishers, 1992), #40.

[3]StudyLight.org, definition of Greek word translated "baptize". http://www.studylight.org/isb/view. cgi? number=907.

[4]Spiros Zodhiates, *The Complete Word Study Dictionary: New Testament*, #1746.

[5]James Strong, *Exhaustive Concordance of the Bible,* "Greek Dictionary of the New Testament," #1411.

5 – Resurrection Life Empowers You

[1]Ibid., #4152.

[2]StudyLight.org, definition of Greek word translated "gifts". http://www.studylight.org/isb/view. cgi? number=5486.

6 – Resurrection Life Enlightens You

[1]Spiros Zodhiates, *The Complete Word Study Dictionary: New Testament*, #3339.

7 – Resurrection Life Quickens You

[1]StudyLight.org, definition of Greek word translated "alive". http://www.studylight.org/isb/view. cgi? number=2227.

Endnotes

8 – Resurrection Life Lifts You

[1]James Strong, *Exhaustive Concordance of the Bible,* "Greek Dictionary of the New Testament," #5485, #5486.

[2]StudyLight.org, definition of Greek word translated "power". http://www.studylight.org/isb/view. cgi? number=1411.

9 – Resurrection Life Authorizes You

[1]Spiros Zodhiates, *The Complete Word Study Dictionary: New Testament,* #746.

[2]James Strong, *Exhaustive Concordance of the Bible,* "Greek Dictionary of the New Testament," #1849.

[3]Spiros Zodhiates, *The Complete Word Study Dictionary: New Testament,* #1411.

[4]Ibid., #2963.

PRAYER OF SALVATION

God loves you—no matter who you are, no matter what your past. God loves you so much that He gave His one and only begotten Son for you. The Bible tells us that "...whoever believes in Him shall not perish but have eternal life" (John 3:16 NIV). Jesus laid down His life and rose again so that we could spend eternity with Him in heaven and experience His absolute best on earth. If you would like to receive Jesus into your life, say the following prayer out loud and mean it from your heart.

Heavenly Father, I come to You admitting that I am a sinner. Right now, I choose to turn away from sin, and I ask You to cleanse me of all unrighteousness. I believe that Your Son, Jesus, died on the cross to take away my sins. I also believe that He rose again from the dead so that I might be forgiven of my sins and made righteous through faith in Him. I call upon the name of Jesus Christ to be the Savior and Lord of my life. Jesus, I choose to follow You and ask that You fill me with the power of the Holy Spirit. I declare that right now I am a child of God. I am free from sin and full of the righteousness of God. I am saved in Jesus' name. Amen.

If you prayed this prayer to receive Jesus Christ as your Savior for the first time, please contact us on the Web at **www.harrisonhouse.com** to receive a free book.

Or you may write to us at
Harrison House • P.O. Box 35035 • Tulsa, Oklahoma 74153